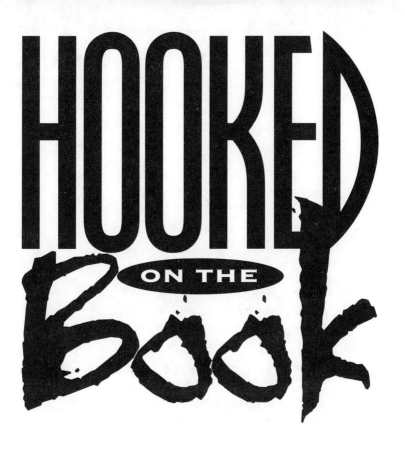

TOM JOHNSON

ZondervanPublishingHouse

Grand Rapids, Michigan

A Division of HarperCollinsPublishers

Hooked on the Book
Copyright © 1996 by Thomas E. Johnson

Requests for information should be addressed to:

📖 Zondervan Publishing House
Grand Rapids, Michigan 49530

Library of Congress Cataloging-in-Publication Data

Johnson, Tom, 1957–.
   Hooked on the book : devotions to help you get the most out of the greatest
book ever written / Tom Johnson.
     p.   cm.
   Summary: Presents thirteen weeks of daily Bible readings with discussions that
help explain the passages and put them into practice.
   ISBN: 0-310-20499-2 (pbk.)
   1. Teenagers—Prayer-books and devotions—English. 2. Devotional calendars.
[1. Prayer books and devotions. 2. Christian life.] I. Title.
BV4850.J65   1996
242'.63—dc 20   96–24535
                                                     CIP
                                                     AC

Interior design by Sue Vandenberg Koppenol

Printed in the United States of America

98 99 00 01 02 03/❖ DH/ 10 9 8 7 6 5 4

To the memory of my father,
whom I never gave enough credit.

INTRODUCTION

First, a word from your sponsor.

The whole point of this book is to better acquaint you with the Bible. You know, the Bible really is the greatest book ever written. But sometimes it can seem like a tough nut to crack. We look at that thick, leather-bound volume on the coffee table or the nightstand or on top of the piano, and we shudder. There it is—all 66 books, 1,189 chapters, 31,173 verses, and 774,746 words of it, written thousands of years ago. And we're clueless. How can we possibly understand it?

Well, it can be done. And *understanding* will be our goal. We won't be plodding through the Bible verse by verse, getting bogged down in nitpicky theological issues. We're going to assume that the Bible is a practical book, applicable to real life. We're going to take a look at the ideas it presents and how we can work those ideas into our own lives. And we're going to have some fun along the way. Trust me.

How to get the most out of the Bible and this book? Here are some suggestions:

1. Choose a version of the Bible that helps you understand what you are reading. Your pastor or youth leader can suggest a readable and reliable version, if you don't already have one.

2. Make sure the Bible you use is a study Bible. This devotional book is just a starting point. A good study Bible will give you lots of extra "helps," like history, outlines, commentary, and cross-references to help you see how the Bible hangs together as a whole. All this stuff will help you "go deeper."

3. Try to read the Bible every day; make it a regular habit. This doesn't have to be a legalistic ball and chain around your neck. Once you're into it, reading the Bible can become as important to you as eating and sleeping.

4. Get involved with what you read. Don't simply read the words (or worse, skip the Scripture passage entirely and just read the devotional—that's cheating). Ask yourself, "What is this passage saying?" And then, "What is it saying to *me*?" Try keeping a journal of your thoughts.

5. Ask the Holy Spirit to help you understand what you've read and apply it to your life. That's the whole idea.

6. Don't get discouraged if you miss a few days—or weeks. Just get back at it. If you don't always understand what you read, welcome to the club—everybody has trouble with certain parts of the Bible. Like I said, it can be a tough nut to crack. Write down your questions and discuss them with your youth leader and other Christian friends.

Because the Bible is God's Word, each page can tell you something about him, about his creation and what he expects of you. It will make you realize that God is a real person who is at work in the world. And it will make you look forward, even more, to the time when you'll see him as he is, in all his power and splendor.

Tom Johnson

WEEK
ONE

Week One: SUNDAY

God: The Only Game in Town

Take a Look: Psalm 104

> *"I am the LORD, and there is no other."*
> *Isaiah 45:5*

OK, I apologize. I did give you a pretty good slug of Scripture to read the first time out. The readings won't all be this long. But Psalm 104 praises God's power and character, and since it's Sunday, I thought it might be nice to spend a little more time thinking about him.

God. His name alone brings to mind a whole bunch of images. What do *you* think of? An old man with a white beard? A king on a throne? Outer space?

The fact that God exists "somewhere out there" brings up a lot of questions. For example, what does he look like? If humankind was created in God's image, does that mean God looks like us, only three miles taller? Does he sit on an actual throne? What's heaven like? Does God live in a separate section of town?

What does he do all day? Float around the universe? Judge the nations? Answer prayers? What does he do in his spare time? Watch *Beverly Hills, 90210*?

We won't know the answer to any of these questions until we go to heaven and meet God or until he makes a guest appearance on *Lifestyles of the Rich and Famous,* which probably won't be anytime soon. You see, it doesn't work to think of God in strictly human terms, because he's bigger and more awesome than anything our finite earthly minds can dream up.

So where does that leave us? Separated from a God who vaguely resembles the shapeless, cosmic clouds of superintelligent energy that Captain Kirk and the gang aboard the U.S.S. *Enterprise* used to run into? Nope. God wants us to know him, and he's gone to a lot of trouble to reveal himself, kindly reducing his incredibly vast self to terms we can understand.

Look around. Something tells you that the universe didn't just show up one day on its own, like the zit that appears the day they're taking yearbook pictures. Creation is just too impressive to be an accident. The guy who wrote Psalm 104 was really excited about the fact that in nature, God is dropping hints about himself—big ones—that tell us he's smart, powerful, and likes variety. We're dealing with a real personality here.

The Bible also shows God to us, but not by cranking out a list of cut-and-dried facts about him. It shows us God in action. First he creates the world, and then he starts unfolding a plan for his creation, including an all-important backup when his creatures fail. The master stroke in his plan? He sends Jesus into the world to bring humankind a second chance, a new way to live, a way to become God's people again.

So what am I leading up to? Simply this: If you're using this book to get to know God better, great! He's inviting you to do just that, and every Sunday for the next thirteen weeks we'll look at another piece in the puzzle of his nature. Just remember—he wants you to know *him,* not just about him. That can be scary, because the more you discover about God, the more you'll discover about yourself and how much you need him. It isn't easy, but stick with it—you're in good hands.

Week One: MONDAY

Talking Back, Part One

Take a Look: Psalm 43

> *"If you believe, you will receive whatever you ask for in prayer."*
>
> *Matthew 21:22*

"Hello, this is God. I'm sorry I'm not in right now. At the tone, leave your name and message, and I'll get back to you as soon as possible."

Ridiculous, right? God doesn't have an answering machine. He doesn't take naps, go on vacation, or get too busy to take our calls. Still, sometimes when we pray, it seems that God is very far away.

Prayer is important. It's key to our daily devotional time. God talks to us through his Word, and we need to "talk back"—to keep the conversation going. Communication is basic to any relationship, including your relationship with God. In the next few days, we'll try to get better at it—kind of a prayer warm-up.

One of the first prayers I ever learned was a rhyming bedtime prayer my parents said with me. That one got to be pretty automatic. But when I was older and realized more about the meaning of a commitment to Christ, praying became more thoughtful and also harder to do. In Matthew 21:22, Jesus says, "If you believe, you will receive whatever you ask for in prayer." When I prayed by myself or even in a group of other Christians, I always wondered if my faith was strong enough. Were my motives pure? Did I believe that what I was praying for could really happen by God's power?

That kind of self-evaluation can be good once in a while, but if it turns into chronic doubt, we're in trouble.

What good can prayer do if God seems distant and we can't trust our own sincerity?

The key to getting out of this rut is to stop thinking of prayer as merely asking God for *things*. It *is* that, but the Bible suggests that it's much more than that. Prayer is a way of relating to God, getting to know him better.

The author of Psalm 43 writes about being oppressed by his enemies. Right after that, he mentions a strong desire to go to God and worship him. He wants an encounter with God's true personality. Have you ever felt like that? Maybe when you're down or disappointed or you're struggling with a problem and can't even think straight, you'd like to go to someone who is all truth and light—not to ask for anything but simply to enjoy the rest and comfort of being with him.

We can do that through prayer. But we have to start by thinking of prayer not as sending God a wish list but rather as coming into his majestic presence. No kidding. Not just in our imaginations but in actual fact. And then taking the opportunity to praise him, as the writer of Psalm 43 does.

This kind of private worship is the true reason God created us in the first place. And it will give us greater confidence when we do make specific requests of him.

More tomorrow. Till then, pray first for God's presence, then for your needs.

Week One: TUESDAY

Talking Back, Part Two

Take a Look: Psalm 92

> *I sing for joy at the works of your hands.*
>
> *Psalm 92:4*

The concert has just ended. You've heard your favorite performer live for the first time, and you decide to do something daring—go for an autograph.

You stand outside the stage door. After an eternity, he finally emerges and you see him face-to-face. A weird feeling—a mixture of awe and adrenaline—shoots through you. It's really him, up close and larger than life.

You hand him your autograph book and a pen, asking him to sign. "It's for my sister," you say, trying to be cool.

But you can't hold it in forever. "I'm your biggest fan! I have all your albums! You're the greatest!" you gush. "When do you think your new album will go platinum?" you ask, as if you were some music industry colleague.

He signs and hands the book back to you. "Soon." He smiles and gets into his limousine.

You don't want the moment to end. The voice on the CD has just become a real, breathing, touchable person.

Your devotional time is the path to having that kind of stage door experience with God. Yesterday we talked about prayer as coming into God's presence. But what do you do once you're there, to feel that real, live closeness with him? Take your cues from the writer of Psalm 92. He understood God's greatness and really talked it up.

Meditate. Concentrate on who God is. Try making a list of his attributes as you read your Bible, and think about what they mean to you. Then think about what God has done—his "greatest hits," so to speak. Let your mind go wild—God's creation is full of marvels. Think of what he has done for you in giving you life and a world to enjoy.

Then tell God how great it all is. Out loud. Enjoy this. Revel in it. Think of all the terrific possibilities the power of God suggests.

Be honest. Absolutely honest. It's just you and God now, and he knows what you're thinking, anyway. Why not say it? If you feel tired and lazy, tell him. If you're so happy about something that you think you'll bust, let 'er rip! Say exactly what you think and feel. Take away the barrier of pretending, and God will seem closer.

Be creative. The writer of Psalm 92 talks about praising God with "the ten-stringed lyre and the melody of the harp" (v. 3). Even if your musical talent is marginal, God still loves a "joyful noise." So give him the best concert you can cook up, even if it's just humming a favorite praise song. Make this an offering to him. Treat him like the real person he is, and he will become more real to you.

Of course, you won't be able to put on a big production all the time. But meeting God in this way on a regular basis will make all of your praying more genuine. You'll feel that you're getting to know a real friend.

Week One: WEDNESDAY

A Change in the Flight Plan

Take a Look: Psalm 107:1–9

He led them by a straight way to a city where they could settle.

Psalm 107:7

Today's Scripture verse reminds us to seek God's guidance. It's an important reminder, because sometimes we don't think about his guidance until we desperately need it.

My friends Kevin and Greg and I once flew from Lincoln, Nebraska, to Billings, Montana, in a small plane. Kevin was our pilot, and although he was very good, he only had a visual flight rating—he hadn't been trained to fly using only the cockpit instruments. That meant that he could only fly in good weather—when he could clearly see landmarks and other planes in the area. And flying through clouds was a definite no-no. So when we ran into a snow-storm over Casper, Wyoming, we were forced to land and stay overnight.

The next day was cold, bright, and clear. Kevin got a good report from the National Weather Service—clear skies all the way from Casper to Billings. Kevin filed his flight plan and we took off. Everything was going great.

But somewhere in the Rocky Mountains, the weather changed unexpectedly. We found ourselves in dense cloud cover. Visibility: zero. Kevin didn't have the training to climb out of the clouds, using instruments only. And we couldn't fly any lower, because of the mountains. I looked down through my backseat window and could barely see the tops of pine trees dotting the peaks and valleys below. I glanced up at Kevin, who was feverishly checking his flight maps to make sure no especially high mountain peaks were in our way. Up to that point, I had lived a pretty uneventful life. But now it crossed my mind that we could crash and die. I started to pray. Hard.

Kevin radioed a "Mayday" call to the Billings control tower. An air traffic controller would have to "talk us down" to the airport. Kevin steered, tensely watching his instruments as the small radio speaker on the instrument panel squawked flight instructions: "Maintain altitude … turn … descend." On we flew into the unending whiteness, trusting the controller to help us avoid smacking into a mountainside.

Finally we got the go-ahead for our approach. Dropping out of the clouds, we found the runway directly beneath us. The tower guided us to a perfect landing.

We had been in a real fix, but the air traffic controller didn't hassle us for getting into trouble. He just gave us the help we needed. That's how God is. It's why the psalmist wrote Psalm 107. When we don't know where we are, we can cry out to the Lord, and he'll deliver us from our distress (v. 6).

Remember: God wants you to reach your destination in one piece. Ask him to show you the way.

Week One: THURSDAY

A Serious Game

Take a Look: Genesis 3:1–19

This is love for God: to obey his commands.
1 John 5:3

The story of Adam and Eve's fall into sin is pretty familiar. In fact, you've probably heard it a hundred times. God created a perfect Garden of Eden and then made a man and a woman to live there. His rules for them were clear: "Eat all you want from any tree in the garden, but don't eat from the tree in the middle of the garden—the Tree of Knowledge of Good and Evil. Touch that and you're history."

Of course, you know what happened. Eve was tempted, disobeyed, and got Adam to go along. They paid a big price.

It reminds me of something actress Justine Bateman said a few years ago. Remember her? She played Mallory on the old *Family Ties* TV show. "Life is basically a game," she told a reporter for *TV Guide*. "If you know how to get what you want by playing the rules, you'll go far. But if you're constantly trying to go against that, you're in for a long journey."

Not a bad philosophy, as far as it goes. Eve could have profited from it. The catch is, God didn't create human beings just so we could get things. He created us out of love, to have a loving relationship with him and enjoy all of what that means. He gave us rules to live by—through the Bible—to maximize that close, loving relationship. And because he knew we'd break his rules, he sent his Son to die for us.

So here's the question for today: are you "playing by the rules" to get what you want, or are you obeying God because you love him? I'm not trying to lay a guilt trip on you. I'm just asking. Because this goes to the heart of what it means to be a Christian. Jesus said it himself: "If you love me, you will obey what I command" (John 14:15).

Love and obedience go together.

Week One: FRIDAY

Reaching

Take a Look: Genesis 11:1–9

"Come, let us build ourselves a city, with a tower that reaches to the heavens."

Genesis 11:4

For over two decades, Sears Tower in Chicago—at over 1,400 feet—has been the world's tallest building. So far, nobody's topped it. But architects and planners have been doing some dreaming, and some cloud-piercing building designs have been talked about.

For instance, the original design for the Chicago World Trade Center would have dwarfed the current big guy, Sears Tower, by reaching to a height of 2,500 feet. In addition to office, retail, and restaurant space, the plan featured 800 apartments, 2,400 hotel rooms, three theaters, and a stellar observatory at the top.

The prize, though, goes to architect Robert Sobel of New York. The tower he'd like to build in Houston, Texas (where they do everything bigger), would be 6,864 feet high (1.3 miles!). It would be a place where you could live, work, shop, exercise, and entertain yourself, without having to leave the building. Ever.

Sound familiar? After the Flood, the descendants of Noah started a building enterprise—the Tower of Babel—but God stopped them. Why? Because they were trying to build a tower high enough to get to heaven on their own?

That's a popular misconception, but no. Actually, the people were disobeying a direct order. In Genesis 9:1, God had told them to "be fruitful and increase in number and fill the earth." But instead of scattering and repopulating the whole world, they chose to stick together. They were probably thinking, *This is a nice place. Let's all just stay here and build a great civilization.* The problem was that they were isolating themselves, when God wanted them to spread out; he had work for them to do. He ended up confusing their language so they would be forced to scatter into the world.

Those people in Genesis remind me of some Christians today. They are so afraid of the world that they isolate themselves, spending all their time at church and with other Christians. They order their lives so they don't have to leave their Christian ivory tower. Ever.

But the lesson of Genesis 11, for us, is that God wants his people to reach out into the world—this time not to repopulate it but to make new disciples of Jesus Christ.

Ask God right now for the strength to go out and represent him in your world.

Week One: SATURDAY

God Can Use Anybody: Peter

Take a Look: Luke 6:12–16; Matthew 16:13–23

Peter answered, "You are the Christ."

Mark 8:29

Since we'll be taking Sundays to concentrate on what God is like, I thought we'd use Saturdays to get the human angle on how God works in the world. To do that, we'll get to know some special people in the life of Jesus—the apostles.

The word *apostle* means "a delegate"—a person who is sent out to represent someone, like an ambassador to a foreign country. Jesus picked twelve men to be his representatives in the world. You'll find all their names in today's reading in Luke.

As you get to know these guys, you may start to wonder if Jesus should have had his head examined for picking them. They weren't all that bright, and a lot of them had quirks, flaws, and weaknesses that got in the way of what Jesus was trying to do. And the chief *quirkmeister* was Peter.

Peter was an impulsive loudmouth. No question about it. He spoke first and asked questions later. And he was fickle. He was the guy in Matthew 16 who was so certain that Jesus was the Messiah. Then, a few verses later, he was trying to talk Jesus out of going to Jerusalem to die. Peter had heard Jesus tell the multitudes to turn the other cheek when persecuted. But it was he who wounded a servant with his sword when Jesus was arrested. Peter said he would always be true-blue. Later, after Jesus' arrest, Peter denied that he ever knew his Lord.

But something happened to Peter. After Jesus' resurrection, the former wise guy was truly changed. The reality of Christ's true identity and power made Peter see life in a new way. He became one of the hardest workers, and strongest leaders, in the church. He didn't lose his flaws; God just turned them around into strengths. Sure, Peter could be a brute. But what he sometimes lacked in tact and judgment, he made up for in energy and enthusiasm.

Peter reminds me of Tim, a friend of mine. He was what I call a *chucklehead*. He was always talking, butting in, making a joke at the most inappropriate times. He embarrassed himself a lot. But in spite of all that—probably *because* of it—he was great with kids and, as a kind of freelance youth pastor, turned our church's dead youth-group into a going, growing thing. His weakness became a plus when he put it to work for God.

Ever feel like an absolute geek? Peter's example can give hope to anybody who ever felt inadequate. He's proof that God really can use anybody.

How can he use *you*?

More next Saturday.

WEEK
TWO

Week Two: SUNDAY

God: All-Powerful

Take a Look: Ezekiel 37:1–14

> *"With God all things are possible."*
> Matthew 19:26

When we talk about God being all-powerful, we often think about him doing big, historic things—creating the stars and the planets, destroying the world with the Flood, raising Jesus from the dead, that kind of thing. But there's another way to think of God's power, and I'll talk more about it in a moment. First, a word about recycling.

You know, next to air and water, garbage may be turning into the world's most abundant resource; it's easy to produce but harder to get rid of. In fact, many cities in North America are running out of landfill space to put it in.

Where to put the trash? Well, we can't sweep it under the rug, obviously. But there's a growing industry dealing with the problem. New facilities are recycling garbage cheaply and safely. At a plant in Minnesota, for example, huge machines separate waste material by size, and employees extract aluminum cans, plastics, and cardboard from garbage chugging by on conveyor belts (and you think you hate *your* job sometimes!). The plant then presses paper and organic stuff into burnable fuel pellets that can be sold as coal and gas substitutes. It's pretty amazing, really, that something we once thought was worthless actually turns out to be a valuable resource. Recycling is a smart thing to do. I hope you're doing it.

Now back to our story. In today's reading, we see a vision of the prophet Ezekiel, who ministered to the people of Israel after they were exiled to Babylon. His message to them was that their rebellion against God had got them into this mess and that the goodness of God would get them out.

In the vision, God takes Ezekiel into a valley full of bones. It's an image of death and stillness, like a mass grave or a battlefield where thousands of soldiers have fallen. This image is a symbol of Israel, broken and defeated. But God causes the bones to come together. Muscles form on those dead bones, skin covers them, and he breathes life into them. It's God's way of illustrating his promised revival of the nation.

It also illustrates the point I want to make about God's power: God is in the recycling business. No matter how stupidly I mess up my life or throw away my opportunities, he can take my "garbage" and make something useful out of it, breathing new life into me in the process.

To me that's real power. Sure, God created the universe, but he did that all by himself, without me around to screw it up. It's what he's able to do with what I've ruined that really impresses me.

Feel like a bonehead sometimes—broken, defeated, like you'll never get it together? With God, all things are possible. Believe it.

Week Two: MONDAY

Making Some Noise

Take a Look: Joshua 6:1–20

> *"Whatever you have commanded us we will do, and wherever you send us we will go."*
>
> *Joshua 1:16*

Yesterday we talked about the garbage crisis. But did you know that some scientists say noise pollution—the unending racket we create with industry, traffic, loud music, and talking too much—may be a problem that's growing even faster?

According to the *Guinness Book of World Records*, though, it could be worse. The loudest noise ever created in a laboratory was reported by NASA in 1965. A 48-foot steel-and-concrete horn in Huntsville, Alabama, belted out a whopping 210 decibels—that's the equivalent of cranking 400,000 watts out of your stereo. The force of the sound was great enough to bore holes in solid materials.

I only bring it up because simple noise is sometimes given the credit for Joshua's successful attack on the walls of Jericho. You usually hear this from people who want to pass off the miracles of the Bible as easily explainable, natural events.

Here's the reasoning I once heard: "The walls of Jericho weren't really built all that well. The people's constant tramping around the walls for seven days caused the foundations to destabilize. On the seventh day, the trumpets and shouting created vibrations that shook the walls and made them crumble." As if to say, like the hero in a scary movie, "See? There's a perfectly logical explanation for all this." Ha.

The truth is, it wasn't the people's walking or horn blowing or shouting that made the walls fall down. It was their *obedience* and God's *power*.

Back in the first chapter of the book of Joshua, when God made Joshua the leader of Israel after Moses died, the people promised to go wherever, and do whatever, Joshua said. And God's instructions to Joshua about taking Jericho were very precise. Notice that nobody questioned those instructions, as odd as they must have sounded; they were followed to the letter. The people of Israel knew that when they obeyed God, awesome things could happen.

Sometimes when we're really trying to achieve and grow—at school or in our relationships, for example—I think God makes us take the long way around, to test our obedience and endurance. If you think God is making you jump through unnecessary hoops to get to your goal, try to jump through just one more. You may be stunned by the results.

Week Two: TUESDAY

Don't Be Afraid

Take a Look: Psalm 23

"Do not fear, for I am with you."

Isaiah 41:10

While he was attending college in Chicago, my brother Paul took a job as a night watchman in a mortuary. You know, a funeral home. For me, doing night duty in a large place of business all by myself would be creepy enough. But in a mortuary? With dead people lying around, deliveries at all hours of the night (folks just don't have the courtesy to die between eight and five daily), and a body preparation table in the basement? Not me, buddy.

Well, my brother did it, but not without a few second thoughts of his own. The first thing he did when he got the job was to check out some library books on how to handle fear. The place gave him the creeps, too.

But what was he really afraid of? The invasion of the body snatchers? Dr. Frankenstein and Igor dropping by for a take-out order? I'm not sure he knew, exactly. He probably just feared the unknown.

Fear is an emotional reaction triggered by the belief that we'll be deprived of something important to us—our lives, our health, our possessions, our security. In a way, it's a reaction against any kind of unexpected change. We'd rather be in control.

Some fear isn't all bad; it can be a motivator, a survival mechanism, like when you meet a bear in the woods (I *hate* it when that happens). Your fear reaction kicks in, and a rush of adrenaline tightens your muscles and makes you more alert, ready for what comes next.

But most of the time fear is bad news. What are you afraid of? Trying out for the school play? Being turned down for a date? Your parents dying? Being embarrassed in public? Flunking out of school? Talking about your faith? No matter what we're afraid of, our fears can grip us like a vise, paralyzing us, robbing us of happiness and achievement.

What to do about fear? I could dish out a lot of psychological advice here. Instead, I'll tell you something even more important—something David had down when he wrote Psalm 23. If you know God, you've got an edge— he's always with you. Now, you might not think this is much comfort. "Sure, God is everywhere," you say. True. But the great thing about knowing God is that he's your constant resource. Need a friend to talk to? He's there. Need an extra shot of courage? He says, "Those who hope in the LORD . . . will soar on wings like eagles" (Isa. 40:31). Need guidance for an especially terrifying situation? He's got a whole book of it for you, and a Spirit to help you understand how to use it.

Fear can get you going or it can get you down. The key is knowing what you're afraid of, taking positive action, and believing God when he says, "Don't be afraid. I'm always around."

Week Two: WEDNESDAY

Thanks for Everything

Take a Look: Psalm 104

The earth is satisfied by the fruit of his work.
Psalm 104:13

Psalm 104 is more than a mere list of God's creative accomplishments. It's a hymn of praise and thanks. The psalmist is absolutely *juiced* about the terrific wonder and variety of God's creation. It's important to do that regularly —consider what God has done and take time to appreciate it. It reminds you that God is a giver of good things.

Of course, there's an official holiday to do just that— Thanksgiving. When I was growing up, Thanksgiving Day followed a set formula: go to church in the morning, come home, eat turkey and all the trimmings until you're ready to gag, watch football games or holiday specials on TV, chat with relatives, eat again later while still stuffed (but hey, it's Thanksgiving!), play Scrabble with cousins, and go to bed vowing never to eat that much again—at least, not until Christmas. It was one of my favorite holidays.

There came a time when I was sort of embarrassed by the whole thing. I mean, after all, weren't we almost *mocking* all those hungry and homeless people in the world who didn't have it so good? Besides, what did taking a day off from work and school, scarfing down rich food, and goofing off have to do with giving thanks to God?

But now I've come to believe that being thankful isn't just *acknowledging* God's provision and generosity to us but celebrating it—reveling in all the good things he gives us to enjoy. The Thanksgiving Day ritual is a celebration of faith, family, food, and fun—all things God meant for us to experience with delight and, in doing so, want to share with others.

It's all about being a good receiver of God's gifts. It's like when Aunt Hattie knits you a sweater: the best thank-you you can give her is to wear it.

Week Two: THURSDAY

Get Smart

Take a Look: Proverbs 4

> *"Get wisdom. Though it cost all you have, get understanding."*
>
> Proverbs 4:7

One Friday night, I made a quick trip to Des Moines, Iowa, using my boss' car. Out on the open road, I turned on the air conditioner, set the automatic speed control at fifty-five (the speed limit then), and cruised toward Des Moines in style and comfort.

What I didn't know was that the automatic speed mechanism was defective. So it wasn't long before I was stopped and ticketed by an Iowa state trooper—doing sixty-nine!

I had made a costly mistake: instead of taking responsibility for observing the speed limit on the way to Des Moines, I had entrusted the job to a machine that had no moral commitment to obey the law—nor, for that matter, had it any fear of being arrested. It just kept singing its little defective heart out, and *I* got caught. The state trooper didn't seem too impressed with my excuses; he just kept writing out the ticket.

The book of Proverbs is a book of wisdom, written mostly by Israel's King Solomon, one of the wisest people who ever lived. In the first several chapters of the book, he drives home a single message: *Get smart. Pursue knowledge and understanding, and you will live well.* And there's another message between the lines: *You're responsible for your own behavior. Don't depend on anyone else to make your choices or take the consequences for those choices.*

Solomon's wisdom was earned through hard experience. He made a lot of mistakes. He did some great things, like building the temple. But his appetite for power and pleasure—he had hundreds of wives, for example—turned him into a dictator. Toward the end of his life, he was very unhappy. He understood how important and far-reaching his previous choices had been. And he could blame the results on no one but himself.

That's why Solomon says, in Proverbs 4, to avoid bad company and pursue wisdom—*real* wisdom that becomes a part of you, guiding your choices. The more you learn, both mentally and spiritually, the more you'll discover how life is really supposed to work. And then you'll have what it takes to make decisions you won't mind taking the consequences for.

It's good advice. Think about it. Otherwise, you might find yourself on the road to Des Moines.

Week Two: FRIDAY

Great Stuff

Take a Look: Ecclesiastes 5:10–16

> *Here is the conclusion of the matter: Fear God and keep his commandments.*
>
> *Ecclesiastes 12:13*

I have this thing about gadgets. I love 'em. If you ever want to buy me a birthday present, here's a good rule of thumb: if it uses batteries, I'll probably go nuts over it.

I come from a long line of gadgeteers. My dad loved 'em, too. Cameras, radios, tape recorders, chain saws, weed whackers . . . He even had a brief but intense love affair with space heaters, as I recall.

Problem is, most of the time my inherited gadgetmania leads to one thing—clutter. Whenever I get a new toy, I have to find a place to put it. Things are getting a little crowded at my house.

There's my electric can opener, which eliminates the strenuous turning of the wrist that manual openers require. The DustBuster vacuum—it's cordless! Picks up those little messes in seconds. A mixer and a blender—one does what the other won't. A microwave oven with a turntable—no more giving the food a quarter turn in the middle of the cooking cycle. Just set and forget! A VCR, which not only has a handsomely styled, seventeen-function remote control but also has fourteen-day, four-event programmability.

And that's just the beginning. No doubt about it, it's been fun to get *stuff.*

But a while back, something happened to me that I hadn't bargained for. I walked into an electronics store just to browse (gadgetmongers love to browse), and as I looked at the veritable wonderland of TV sets, VCRs, stereos, CD players, and little accessories (my favorite), I realized something: there was nothing in the whole place I needed. Nothing, really, that I even wanted. This was unnerving. Normally I got kind of a rush looking at the merchandise, working the little knobs and buttons, adjusting the color on all the TV sets. But now it seemed like a waste of time even dropping in.

I was experiencing the truth of an ancient Chinese proverb: "Wanting is more desirable than having." Always wanting more, something better, gives me a sense of *possibilities*—that my life can be more fun, more fulfilling, if I can just get more stuff. But then when I finally have it, I realize that it wasn't the stuff I wanted, after all. It was the *possibilities,* the hope of enjoying life more than I do now.

Solomon understood this. Read Ecclesiastes and you'll see a man who had it all—money, fame, power, *stuff.* And he became a disillusioned old man. Fortunately, he came back to the reality of why we're all here: "Fear God and keep his commandments."

Have I reached the end of the line on gadgets? Probably not. But I do know that if I become a captive of my possessions, enslaved to the desire for more, I won't have time to love God *or* keep his commandments. I'll be looking for a place to put my *stuff.*

Week Two: SATURDAY

God Can Use Anybody, the Sequel: Andrew

Take a Look: John 1:35–42

The first thing Andrew did was to find his brother Simon and tell him, "We have found the Messiah."
John 1:41

For my entire life, I have stood in a tall, thin shadow—the shadow of my brother Tim.

Tim is the fifth kid in our family and two years older than I. I'm the sixth, the "baby" (boy, did I get sick of hearing *that* while growing up!). Today Tim is the closest friend I have in the world. But our relationship wasn't always so cozy.

Tim was a born leader—outspoken, hardworking, disciplined. Even when we were in grade school, he was always front and center, running for class offices, making friends with his teachers, pulling the good grades. And I admired him. I wanted to be like him, because his life seemed so effortlessly rewarding. Of course, he was putting out a lot of effort, but it looked easy to me. I was always following his lead, even when I didn't really want to.

As a college freshman, I arrived on campus as "Tim Johnson's little brother." It seemed that many of the things I wanted to accomplish at school, he had already done, with distinction. He still knew how to be at the center of things. When I look back, I can see that my college career was a disaster, because I was constantly trying to imitate Tim and share his experiences, hoping some of his "magic" would rub off on me.

In John 1 we meet Andrew, Peter's brother. Many people don't realize it, but Andrew was Jesus' first disciple. He was the one who brought Peter to Jesus. Of course, we know what happened after that: Peter, with his loud-mouthed, extroverted personality, moved in and tried to run the whole show. If I had been Andrew, I probably would have dropped out of Jesus' inner circle altogether—the bro had stolen the spotlight again.

That's not what Andrew did, though. He didn't seem to care much about being noticed; he was too busy doing the work. And his real talent seemed to be evangelism—bringing people to Jesus. When Jesus fed the five thousand in John 6, it was Andrew who brought the boy with the five loaves and two fish to him. In John 12, when some Greeks wanted a meeting with Jesus, it was Andrew who brought them together. Andrew was really the first missionary, and because of his good work, he became a leader among the disciples, just as Peter did.

Like most people, you're probably standing in the shadow of someone—a parent, a brother or sister, a friend, a classmate—who makes you feel inadequate. But God isn't interested in how much attention you get or how much popularity you have. He's far more interested in how much you're willing to do for him.

No matter how invisible you think you are, you can bring people to Jesus.

WEEK THREE

Week Three: SUNDAY

God: Holy

Take a Look: Isaiah 6:1–8; Matthew 5:43–48

"Holy, holy, holy is the LORD *Almighty; the whole earth is full of his glory."*

Isaiah 6:3

"Be perfect, therefore, as your heavenly Father is perfect."

Matthew 5:48

Language is a funny thing; it's always changing. Words come and go, take on new meanings, or drop out of our conversation completely. Americans are really fickle about *slang* words, especially adjectives. There was a time when *groovy* was the word used to describe something that had previously been called *neat-o*. Later on, *gnarly* replaced *groovy*. And so on.

Well, somewhere along the line, the word *holy* became a joke—or worse, gave people a negative feeling. Ever hear somebody called a "Holy Joe," a "Holy Roller," or "holier-than-thou"? Those phrases are a slam—they describe people (often religious people) who think they're better than others. Then, of course, *holy* became part of people's mild swearing— "holy cow," "holy Moses," or "Holy red snapper, Batman!" Most people just don't take *holy* seriously anymore, and I think it's because they don't know what holiness really is.

In today's reading, Isaiah is brought face-to-face with the holiness of God in the temple. He sees the Lord on his throne, smells the smoke, feels the floor shake at the voices of the seraphim, and immediately becomes a quivering mass of protoplasm. Why? Because he realizes that compared to God, he's lowlife, scum.

But what was he so impressed with? It all comes down to language. The Hebrew word used here for *holy* has several shadings, but it mainly means "set apart, perfect, in a class by itself." When we say God is holy, we're saying he is special—whole, perfect, complete. Isaiah's experience was a little like being sent into a basketball game to play against Michael Jordan—awe-inspiring and a little intimidating. It's painful to compare ourselves with excellence.

Fortunately for Isaiah (and for us), God provides for human inadequacy. When Isaiah was purified with fire by the seraphim, he was no longer shamed by God's perfection but drawn to it. He was willing to go where God wanted him to go. We are purified through Jesus' death on the cross and through the continuing work of the Holy Spirit in our lives.

When Jesus tells us in Matthew 5 to be perfect, he's not expecting that we'll never sin. But he is inviting us to shoot for holiness—maturity, wholeness, and completeness through a growing relationship with him. He wants us to be the best we can be, especially in how we behave toward other people.

For the next two weeks, we'll take a look at God's most famous guidelines for our behavior—the Ten Commandments. Don't chicken out on this; it'll be fun. Meanwhile, remember that *holy* is the best thing you could ever hope to be.

Week Three: MONDAY

Number One

Take a Look: Exodus 20:1–17

> *"You shall have no other gods before me."*
> *Exodus 20:3*

Get the picture: Moses and the people of Israel, who have escaped from slavery in Egypt, have been traveling eastward for about three months. When they reach the Sinai Desert, God makes an announcement to Moses: "In three days, I'm making a special appearance on Mount Sinai. Be there."

So on the third day, Moses goes up the mountain to meet God. The scene is like a bigger version of Isaiah's temple experience—fire and smoke, earthquakes, thunder and lightning. If Moses had brought a kite and a brass key, who knows? He might have discovered electricity.

Why the big show? God has shown up to dictate the first part of the Law—the Ten Commandments. The first rule on the list? "You shall have no other gods before me."

Now, you've probably known somebody who always has to be first—the center of attention, the big cheese. Usually we conclude that people like this are really insecure inside and are out to prove something. So what's God doing here—indulging some kind of divine inferiority complex? Does he have some kind of neurotic need to be worshiped— to be Numero Uno?

Well, the answer is found in what God says before he starts dictating the Big Ten, in verse 2: "I am the LORD your God, who brought you out of Egypt, out of the land of slavery."

You see, it's not as if God showed up late at the party and started telling the band what to play, grabbing for attention. God didn't have anything to prove; he'd already proved himself many times. He had been with the Israelites through thick and thin. He had shown his power in Egypt during the ten plagues, when Pharaoh and the gang had been up to their earlobes in frogs and locusts. God had opened up the Red Sea so the Israelites could cross, and had given the Egyptians a cold bath.

If the people of Israel had to pick a god to whom they could give their absolute loyalty, Jehovah's credentials for the job were excellent. Because everything God does is an expression of who he is—the most powerful and loving being imaginable.

Think of what God has done for you. He has given you life, a world to enjoy, people to love (and who love you), eternal life, and a lot of other stuff I don't even know about. Still, maybe you're sometimes tempted to invest most of your love and attention elsewhere. Because God loves you, he wants you to know and worship him—your only true source of security and hope. What God says is simple: "I am the Lord your God. Stick with me and we'll go places."

Week Three: TUESDAY

Accept No Substitutes

Take a Look: Romans 1:18–25

"You shall not make for yourself an idol."
Exodus 20:4

Stop me if you've heard this one. A little boy is drawing a picture. His mother asks him what he's drawing. "God," he informs her. "But nobody knows what God looks like," Mom says. The kid answers, "They will when I'm finished." Har-har.

Ever been frustrated by the fact that God is invisible? Join the club. Everybody would like to meet God "in the flesh." This heaven-to-earth thing seems unsatisfying sometimes, like trying to have a long-distance relationship by letter with the true love you met at summer camp. You *know* they're there, but they'd be a lot more real to you up close and personal.

I had a few of those post office romances. To deal with the distance, we traded photographs, jewelry, small gifts.

We always thought that having something to touch would make us feel closer. Problem was, those doodads—those pieces of ourselves we gave each other—didn't really satisfy. They only made us more heartsick for the real thing.

In Romans 1, Paul talks about people who supposedly wanted to know and worship God. But they confused God with his creations and ended up worshiping the things he'd created, instead of the Creator. "Wait a minute," you say. "What does that have to do with me? Christians don't worship idols."

Oh, no? What about *church* people who put their faith in a man or in a building or in the pulpit furniture or in the old Bible on the communion table? All these things may "feel like God," because they make some folks feel cozy and safe. But they're really lousy substitutes. That's why God nixes idols, in Exodus 20:4. They're an insult to him, and they only make us heartsick for the real thing.

What do you think of when you hear the words *God, church, faith*? If you think of religious *stuff* instead of a relationship with a *Person,* you may have a few idols rattling around in your spiritual closet.

Week Three: WEDNESDAY

. . . And Don't Wear It Out

Take a Look: Psalm 8

> *"You shall not misuse the name of the Lord your God."*
>
> *Exodus 20:7*

My last name, Johnson, is the second most common name in America. I've often been told that I have a common name, but some people aren't so nice about it. While I lived in Minneapolis, I once heard a guy say, "There are too many Johnsons in this town. I wish I could rip fifty pages of 'em out of the phone book!"

Well, thanks a lot, buddy, I thought. *You're talking about my name here. I like my name. It's important to me. Just because my name isn't Robert Redford or Zbigniew Brzezinski doesn't mean it's any less a part of my identity.*

Names *are* important. Once somebody knows your name, it becomes a part of their whole perception of you. And during biblical times, names were tied up in a person's identity even more than they are today. Often a newborn baby was named for an event that happened around the time of the birth, or for a physical characteristic. That's how Esau got his name, in Genesis 25. *Esau* means "hairy." No doubt about it, Esau was a regular shag carpet. And his hairiness became significant later on (check out the story of Isaac's blessing, in Genesis 27).

God's name is *really* important. "You shall not misuse the name of the LORD your God," he thundered to Moses on Mount Sinai. What does that mean? Well, apparently there was a lot of false swearing going on at the time. Ever hear somebody say, "I swear to God, someday I'll do something-or-other"? People often forget to follow through on promises like that. To which God says, "Look, if you're gonna make phony oaths, don't drag my name into it."

That's one part of it. But the other part is simple carelessness. There were some girls in my junior high school who peppered their conversations with God's name. But it came out as kind of a nasal "Gaaahhhhhhhd!" Anything that was surprising or gross or lame got the "Gaaahhhhhhhd!" treatment. It got old really fast. In high school a lot of guys, when they were angry, routinely asked God to damn certain people or inanimate objects. I have a hunch that the people who use God's name the most may know the least about him.

King David, though, knew God well. And in Psalm 8 he gets to the heart of why we're told not to throw God's name around carelessly: God's name is *majestic.* It's more than just a handle; it identifies the one who created the universe. Blowing off its importance offends God and makes us look stupid.

Look at it this way: how would you like it if somebody yelled your name every time they hit their thumb with a hammer?

Week Three: THURSDAY

Never on Sunday

Take a Look: Mark 2:23–3:6

> *"Remember the Sabbath day by keeping it holy."*
> *Exodus 20:8*

> *"The Sabbath was made for man, not man for the Sabbath."*
> *Mark 2:27*

The fourth commandment reminds us of the importance of observing a day of rest and worship. For the Jews of Moses' time, it was the last day of the week, in honor of the fact that God created the world in six days and rested on the seventh. Christians decided to observe it on the first day of the week, in honor of Christ's resurrection.

Well, lots of cities and towns across America take the fourth commandment very seriously and have passed laws to regulate certain Sunday activities. For example, did you know that in Studley, Virginia, it's against the law to play with a yo-yo in public on the Sabbath—especially while in church or Sunday school? It's true.

How does something that bizarre end up on the law books? Only the good citizens of Studley can answer that question. But it makes me wonder: Was this important enough to write a law about? Were yo-yos really such a threat to the dignity of the Sabbath?

The Pharisees, the religious leaders of Jesus' day, would have loved it. Their Sabbath laws were very strict. On the Sabbath, a Jew couldn't work, make a fire for cooking, buy, sell, or travel. The Pharisees prided themselves on obeying these laws to the letter. In fact, they were so concerned with the *letter* of the law that they forgot its *spirit*.

That's why, in today's reading, when Jesus healed the man with the withered hand, they said, "Aha! Practicing medicine on the Sabbath! Foul! Two shots!" They ignored the fact that the man had been healed, that his life had been changed. Keeping the Sabbath had become such a game to them that they had forgotten the real purpose of the day.

God made the Sabbath so that there would be one day a week when people could take a break from the grind of making a living (or earning a diploma, for that matter), relax, and concentrate on the finer things—like their relationships with God and each other. It wasn't just some arbitrary rule that God came up with. As Jesus said, "The Sabbath was made for man." We need a break. People burn themselves out without it.

How do you spend your Sundays? Too many stressful activities can rob you of the break you need. Use the day to worship God, recharge your batteries, think about the previous week, and prepare mentally for the next one. Your relaxation could take many forms: napping, reading, fishing, sunbathing. There are lots of possibilities. But do something that allows you to get up Monday morning ready for a fresh start.

That's the way to keep the Sabbath holy.

Week Three: FRIDAY

The Guy in the Suit

Take a Look: Ephesians 6:1–4

"Honor your father and your mother."

Exodus 20:12

My dad was what they call a type A: active, driven, absorbed in his work. Eventually his profession started to come before his family. It wasn't that he didn't love us; he was just type A.

I was the youngest of six, and I always felt a distance between Dad and myself. He could be strict. His suit and tie were almost a part of him. He wasn't in touch with new trends or who was hot and who wasn't. Most of all, he seemed hard to pin down. He was always doing something or going somewhere. It was just in his blood.

He was fifty-one when the years of stress, cholesterol, and type A-ness started to catch up with him. The arteries in his heart were clogged, and he needed surgery. At the time, it didn't really faze me. I knew it was my father going under the knife, but I somehow viewed him more as the guy in the blue suit who came around at dinnertime to lay down the law.

Dad recovered well from the surgery, but distance still defined our relationship. Things got worse when I ran into trouble with my grades in college. Dad was on my back a lot. When he had a slight heart attack, I was unconcerned. The distance was widening.

Then something strange happened. While Dad and Mom were on vacation one summer, he wrote me a letter telling me not to worry about finishing school right then if I felt it was impossible—"There might be a better time," he said. For the first time, I felt Dad was respecting my feelings. Loving me. Period. The pressure was off, and our relationship improved.

I began to see my father as others did. Bright. A leader in his profession. A man of integrity who was loved and admired. I remember my outrage when he got fired, basically for telling the truth. He had guts. Our conversations deepened. I was finally seeing the man behind the suit.

A series of heart attacks led to more surgery in February 1986. This time, there had been lots of heart damage, and he never fully recovered. After yet another heart attack, he died on August 4.

Unfortunately, I failed to stay in touch that summer. If I'd known how sick he was, there were lots of things I would have said to him. But my biggest regret was not being there with him and Mom when he was facing the end.

Before my father died, I don't think I understood what it meant to "honor your father and your mother." I know now that it's more than just obedience. It also has to do with *valuing* your parents as people, appreciating them as a source of wisdom and love, and drawing on their maturity and judgment while you're making your own life-shaping decisions.

Thanks to Dad's willingness to love me, period, we had six years together as good friends. I wish now that I had moved first. I wish I had given him more credit as a good human being. I wish I had accepted him, reached out to him, spent more time with him. And I wish life wouldn't go by so quickly.

You won't always have your parents around, either. Is there emotional distance between you and your folks? Look for a way to build some bridges.

Week Three: SATURDAY

God Can Still Use Anybody: John

Take a Look: John 20:1–10

> *Don't let anyone look down on you because you are*
> *young, but set an example for the believers.*
> *1 Timothy 4:12*

In today's Scripture passage, you read the story of Jesus'
resurrection and how the "disciple whom Jesus loved"
reached the empty tomb first (John 20:2–4). That was John.

When it comes to apostles, John is in a class by himself. His special relationship with Jesus set him apart. Consider the following:

John was first a disciple of John the Baptist, who prepared the way for the Messiah.

When John decided to follow Jesus, he quickly became
a member of Jesus' inner circle, and a leader among the disciples. He is mentioned in the biblical accounts of Jesus'
best-known miracles.

At the Last Supper, John "reclined on Jesus' breast" at
the table. Jesus even told him who was going to betray him.
And it was John who, along with James and Peter, was with
Jesus in the Garden of Gethsemane when Judas appeared
with the armed guard to arrest him.

Before he died on the cross, Jesus entrusted his mother, Mary, to John's care.

John's biblical writings—the gospel of John, his three
letters, and the book of Revelation—are considered literary
masterpieces.

John had a long ministry and was the last of Jesus' original twelve disciples to die.

All of this is pretty remarkable. But what makes it especially interesting is one fact about John I haven't mentioned.

He was the youngest of the Twelve. We don't know exactly how old he was, but some scholars have guessed he might have been as young as twenty when he first met Jesus.

Think about it. John was younger—maybe a lot younger—than Jesus' other eleven picks for his team. That fact alone could have shoved him into the background. And yet he had this special relationship with the Lord that made him a key player, with deep spiritual insights.

Why did Jesus take such a liking to John? It may have been *because* John was so young. He was fresh, with his whole life ahead of him. Maybe he was more teachable, not so set in his ways as some of the others. Or maybe Jesus warmed to John's sincere spiritual interest; he was really *looking* for Christ.

Of course, John wasn't perfect. Jesus called him and his brother James "sons of thunder," because of their quick tempers and their aggressiveness. Still, John had started his spiritual quest early, and that gave him a lot of years to grow in Christ.

Maybe Paul was thinking of John when he wrote to Timothy, another young Christian, "Don't let anyone look down on you because you are young, but set an example for the believers." You're never too young to take your faith seriously and become more like Jesus.

WEEK FOUR

Week Four: SUNDAY

God: Just

Take a Look: Proverbs 24

> *Do not fret because of evil men.*
>
> Proverbs 24:19

When God gave Israel the Ten Commandments, he was acting in the role of a teacher, instructing them on the best way to live.

But God isn't only a teacher in the school of life; he's also the principal. He enforces the rules and acts as judge. Breaking the rules—in school or in life—has consequences.

Today's reading tells us that God is *just;* he makes sure that everyone gets what they deserve. But that invites an obvious question: if God is just, how come good people often suffer and bad people seem to get away with murder? Well, read on.

One rainy night, I returned to my apartment to find signs of a break-in. The living room window was open, and the screen—with jagged, vertical rips in it—was on the floor, propped against the wall. I blinked. *That's odd. How'd that screen come off?* Before I could think of an answer, I heard the bedroom door opening. Then footsteps. I was definitely not alone!

I turned to see two young men appear from around the corner and saunter toward the door. I had surprised two burglars inside my apartment! For a second I was stunned. "Hey!" I yelled, indignant, as they strode past and bolted out the door into the darkness. I gave chase—for about ten feet. Then I came to my senses and called 911.

The police arrived, poked around, dusted for fingerprints, and asked a lot of questions, just like on *Dragnet.* In the next few days, I looked at mug shots and viewed a police lineup, complete with two-way mirrors. I was able to identify only one of the men. He was charged with criminal trespassing.

I testified in court two months later. I told the truth, the whole truth, and nothing but the truth. But the defense attorney produced a "witness" who claimed he'd been with the defendant for the whole night in question. Right. It was probably the other guy in my apartment—his accomplice in the crime! The case was dropped.

So my first experience with the criminal justice system was a dud; a criminal went free. I was angry. Still, I had to be thankful. The intruders hadn't had a chance to steal any of my stuff. I hadn't risked my neck trying to stop them. And I had done the right thing by calling the authorities. I chalked it up to experience.

Months later my local paper published a list of people arrested by the FBI for selling stolen goods. At the top of the list? You guessed it—my burglar! This time the charges stuck; he went to jail.

The point of the story is that God's justice is sure—but on his timetable, not ours. Evil will be defeated—maybe not today, maybe not tomorrow, maybe not even in our lifetime. But someday God will deal with evil and evil men. Permanently.

That's why Solomon tells us, "Do not fret because of evil men or be envious of the wicked, for the evil man has no future hope, and the lamp of the wicked will be snuffed out" (Prov. 24:19–20). Eventually God's judgment will fall. In the meantime, my job is to keep on doing good.

Pray now and tell God you trust him to handle the bad guys.

Week Four: MONDAY

Live and Let Live

Take a Look: Genesis 4:1–15

> *"You shall not murder."*
>
> *Exodus 20:13*

Charlie Starkweather was bad news. Back in 1958, in my city of Lincoln, Nebraska, he and his girlfriend, Caril Ann Fugate, murdered eleven people. Three of those people were Fugate's mother, stepfather, and baby sister.

Charlie was nineteen. Caril was fourteen.

The community was shocked almost out of its mind. Over the eight days of the murder spree, people panicked. The National Guard was called out to patrol Lincoln streets. Parents kept their children home from school. Rumors ran wild.

When Starkweather and Fugate were finally caught and brought to trial, Caril was sentenced to life in prison. Charlie went to the electric chair. It was a pretty sickening story.

But what's even more sickening is this: back in the fifties, a crime like this shocked and outraged the whole country; today a lot more than eleven people are murdered in American cities every weekend, and we've become so used to it, we hardly feel a thing.

It's sickening, all right. And scary. When we stop being shocked at violence, we start to devalue human life.

The sixth commandment is short and simple: "You shall not murder." And from the story of Cain and Abel, in today's Scripture reading, the Bible makes it clear that taking a human life is one of the worst things you can do.

Why? Well, for one thing, humans are created in God's image. As God's best creations, we share with him a unique worth and dignity. But secondly—and just as important—

God always roots for life, with all its potentials and problems. "I have come that they may have life, and have it to the full," Jesus said of his sheep, in John 10:10. Jesus laid down his own life to save ours. He wants our lives to work, to be significant and fulfilling.

Ever hear the expression, "While there's life, there's hope"? Among other things, this means that as long as a person is conscious and breathing, they still have a chance to get their life together, to become the person God wants them to be. But when somebody cuts that life short, hope goes down the tubes.

The Bible warns that the impulse to kill starts small, with our inner feelings: "Anyone who hates his brother is a murderer" (1 John 3:15). This is what happened to Cain. His envy and hatred of Abel led to actions he probably didn't think he would ever commit. And when our hearts are full of hate, *we* can hurt people in lots of ways *short* of murder.

On the other hand, when we show love to others or when we simply get along peacefully with them, we show that we value their lives and affirm their potential for good.

Now, you may easily go through your entire life without actually murdering anybody. But there's a lot more to obeying the sixth commandment than simply not taking someone's life. How about choosing to love—even the guy who steals your best girl, or vice versa—applauding life, hanging on to hope, and respecting the God-given potential in other people?

Week Four: TUESDAY

No Cheating

Take a Look: Proverbs 6:20–35

> *"You shall not commit adultery."*
> *Exodus 20:14*

Finally . . . a subject you've likely been waiting for: SEX.

You've probably heard plenty about putting off having a sexual relationship until you're married. That's excellent advice, not to mention an outright command from the Scriptures. There can be very real consequences to *not* waiting: bruised emotions, sexually transmitted diseases, pregnancy, to name only a few.

All this talk about rules and consequences doesn't mean sex in itself is bad. Let's get that straight right away. Sex is *good*. God created it for human beings to enjoy. It's one of his best ideas. But sex is also complicated. The Bible says it's too good and too complicated to be treated casually.

Your sexual identity—male or female—is a big part of your personality. And you express it in a lot of nonphysical ways. It influences how you think and feel. It affects your views of other people and situations. It's something you *are.*

Today's Scripture reading and the seventh commandment aren't about abstaining from sex *before* marriage; they're about how we treat sex *after* marriage. Now, you'd think that when people get married, all their sexual problems will be settled; they'll have a mate for life. Unfortunately, in our imperfect world, a lot of marriages—and sexual relationships within marriages—break down. There are a million reasons why this happens, but it often boils down to married people not valuing each other or not really being committed to each other in the first place.

Sometimes people in unfulfilling marriages look elsewhere for a little comfort, understanding, and physical affection. And that's when adultery enters the picture—sexual relations between a married person and someone he or she isn't married to.

Like premarital sex, adultery has consequences. Big ones. When someone commits adultery, things change, usually permanently. Adultery is a betrayal, a stab to the heart. People who once trusted each other don't anymore.

A couple who had been "one flesh" are cut in two. It often means the end of a marriage—maybe two marriages.

There's no escaping the consequences, either. "Can a man scoop fire into his lap without his clothes being burned? Can a man walk on hot coals without his feet being scorched?" (Prov. 6:27–28). Fooling around with someone else's husband or wife is playing with fire.

Perhaps adultery wouldn't be such a big deal if the human sex drive were just another physical appetite. But sexuality is all wrapped up with what it means to be human. And God wants human beings to be whole and undamaged.

Married sex can be one of the great joys of your life. It's a gift; don't "share" it with anyone else.

Week Four: WEDNESDAY

Sticky Fingers

Take a Look: Acts 4:32–5:11

> *"You shall not steal."*
>
> *Exodus 20:15*

Ever walk into a store and see a sign that says, "Shoplifters will be prosecuted"? Apparently, a lot of businesspeople believe in the eighth commandment. Shoplifting is a big problem; when store owners lose merchandise to theft, they have to raise their prices to make up the loss. So everybody suffers.

But did you know that shoplifting is only part of the problem? A lot of stealing from businesses isn't done by customers. It's done by employees.

I recently saw a TV news show on this topic. A hidden camera had videotaped cashiers, salespeople, and stockroom workers using clever tricks to rip off their employers—tearing the tags off clothes and jewelry and wearing them out of the store; throwing merchandise out the back door to their friends; failing to ring up purchases at the cash register, then stuffing the customers' money into their own pockets. As I watched, I got angrier by the minute. *How could these people justify their actions?* I thought. *Who do they think they are?*

One employee, speaking on camera (with his face in the shadows, of course), bragged about stealing over sixty thousand dollars' worth of merchandise from companies he'd worked for. "Look," he said, "the only one I'm hurting is a big corporation that's making enough money already. If I don't do it, somebody else will."

That's the way most people justify stealing—they make the victim invisible. This kind of thief wouldn't think of knocking a lady down on the street and grabbing her purse; that's stealing from a real person. But when the victim is faceless—"a big corporation," for example—their consciences aren't bothered as much.

In today's Scripture reading, Ananias and Sapphira agreed to sell their property and give the money to the church. It was a way of sharing with the poor. But they didn't give the apostles all of the money; they held back some for themselves.

I can just hear them rationalizing this decision to each other: "What's the harm? We're still making a big contribution to the church. We're not hurting anybody. Who has to know?"

But God knew. The apostles sensed it. And Ananias and Sapphira paid for their dishonesty with their lives. They tried to make the victim—the church—invisible. But God sees all victims.

Stealing is always a lie. Spending money and possessing things that don't really belong to us tells a phony story about what we've earned for ourselves and deprives others of what they've earned.

There are lots of subtle ways to steal—fudging on your time card at work or loafing on the job; getting (and keeping) too much change at the checkout counter; using somebody's car and not paying them for the gas you've used; hiding a towel in your gym bag and taking it out of the locker room ...

The list could go on, but you don't really need a list to know when you're stealing. Just listen to God's Spirit.

Week Four: THURSDAY

Passing the Buck

Take a Look: Acts 6:8–15; 7:51–60

"You shall not give false testimony against your neighbor."

Exodus 20:16

When the city of Minneapolis, Minnesota, finally decided to build a domed stadium for its professional sports teams, fans were ecstatic. No more rained-out Twins baseball games. No more freezing your backside during late-season Vikings football games. Fans could enjoy the sports indoors, in climate-controlled comfort.

But the Hubert H. Humphrey Metrodome wasn't perfect. In fact, visiting baseball teams absolutely hated the park. They said that the lighting glared in their eyes, the white fabric roof made it hard to see fly balls, and the place was so small, the sound of the crowd was deafening. It was hard to adjust to.

So when the Minnesota Twins beat the St. Louis Cardinals to win the World Series title in 1987, a lot of St. Louis fans (and players) cried foul. "It wasn't fair to make the Cardinals play in a weird stadium like that," they said. "The Metrodome is like a big booby trap for visiting teams. Nobody can play well in that place. The Twins didn't deserve the title. They didn't win; that stupid ballpark did!"

The truth was, St. Louis had lost and the fans couldn't accept their team's defeat. So they put the blame on the ballpark. And that's often what "giving false testimony" amounts to—shifting blame. We don't want to accept responsibility for our own failures, so we blame something—or somebody—else.

That's what happened to Stephen in today's reading. He was having a really powerful ministry among the people, and the Jewish leaders resented it. So they got some people to make false charges about him, and he was dragged before the religious council, the Sanhedrin. Before the council, he delivered a stinging, in-your-face sermon about their stubborn unbelief. Since they couldn't answer his arguments, they took him out and stoned him to death. They were threatened by the truth, so they made Stephen pay.

Can you think of a time when you blamed somebody else for something that was your own fault? Like when you broke something in the house and blamed it on your little brother? "Giving false testimony" goes beyond simple lying. It can destroy people and their reputations. You're better off, in the long run, to admit your faults and tell the truth.

Truth. It's one of the most important things in the world. And it's what the ninth commandment is all about.

Week Four: FRIDAY

Don't Even Think about It

Take a Look: Colossians 3:1–17

Set your minds on things above, not on earthly things.
Colossians 3:2

"You shall not covet."
Exodus 20:17

Well, can you believe it? We're almost through all of the Ten Commandments. And you've survived.

It hasn't been such a bad trip, has it? It's even easy to see a pattern: the first four commandments talk about how we relate to God, and the next five are about how we treat other people. Each commandment is pretty clearly defined, which is nice. Usually, the more clearly the rules are spelled out, the easier they are to obey.

Until today.

You see, the tenth commandment is like the others, but with a twist. While the first nine cover what we *do,* the tenth gets into what we *think.* "You shall not covet"—meaning, "You shall not want what you don't have."

Ouch! Pretty tough, huh? What's wrong with wanting things—a car, new clothes, a nice house someday? And even if it's wrong to *want* 'em, how can you keep from *thinking* about 'em? I don't know about you, but things fly in and out of my mind all day long. What's the deal?

Well, as usual, God knows human beings better than we know ourselves. He knows that all sin starts with a thought. "Each one is tempted when, by his own evil desire, he is dragged away and enticed," says James. "Then, after desire has conceived, it gives birth to sin" (James 1:14–15).

Notice the list in Exodus 20:17: "You shall not covet your neighbor's house ..." (a nice house means status, a symbol of wealth; great to have, but people who value *things* above everything else are really guilty of breaking the first commandment—worshiping something other than God) "... your neighbor's wife ..." (people who fantasize about someone else's spouse may eventually give in to their sexual attraction and violate the seventh commandment—committing adultery) "... or his manservant or maidservant, his ox or donkey, or anything that belongs to your neighbor" (wanting things too much can ultimately lead to stealing—breaking the eighth commandment). See how sin begins with a thought?

Of course, we're always going to want things in our lives. But when simple desires turn into greed and envy, we're in trouble. Fortunately, God gives us an out. In today's Scripture reading, Paul tells the Colossians that the way to break free of the slavery of materialism and unhealthy emotions is to realize that our lives with Christ are *spiritual*. The only things we can take with us out of this world are our spiritual assets—increased faith, wisdom, honesty, kindness, forgiveness, and love. Concentrating on all of those spiritual things will help us to be content with the material things we already have.

Week Four: SATURDAY

God Can Use Anybody, the Saga Continues: Philip

Take a Look: John 1:43–46; 14:1–14

> *"Whoever acknowledges me before men, I will also acknowledge him before my Father in heaven."*
> *Matthew 10:32*

When I was fifteen, I had the chance to attend a Billy Graham crusade in Minneapolis, held at the grandstand of the Minnesota State Fairgrounds. It was an unforgettable experience. I had seen lots of crusades on television, but this time I got to see all of the behind-the-scenes stuff.

One of things I had always wondered about was what Billy Graham actually said to all those people who went forward at the end. It turned out to be really quite simple: pray to accept Christ; tell someone else about your decision; get involved in a fellowship of believers so you can start to grow spiritually.

Dr. Graham really stressed the "tell someone else" part. Telling someone else about your decision for Christ would make things more final and definite, for one thing. But he was also referring to Matthew 10:32. When we own up to our faith in Christ with the people around us, Christ confirms our faith with God and the angels in heaven. (See Luke 12:8 and Rev. 3:5.)

I bring this up because today we're talking about Philip. Now, this is Philip the apostle. Later on, there was another Philip, who was a deacon in the Jerusalem church. But this Philip was one of the original Twelve.

Philip could be called the "forgotten apostle," I suppose. We really don't know much about him, since he's barely mentioned in the Scriptures. We know nothing definite about his ministry, so he's not remembered for any miracles or great accomplishments. And you don't find many churches or hospitals named after him. In today's Scripture reading from John 14, Philip proved to be just as dense as the rest of the apostles when it came to Jesus' true identity. Aside from being chosen by Jesus, he may have led a pretty unremarkable life.

But Jesus *did* choose him. And in the reading from John 1, we can see that Philip satisfied the requirements for being a real Christian. He believed; he told someone else (Nathanael) that he had found Christ; he became part of Jesus' group of disciples, learning from him. That was enough.

For every Billy Graham in the world, there may be a thousand Philips. Not everybody has great speaking ability or deep spiritual insight or personal charm. But Philip had himself. And that's what he gave to Christ.

Don't worry too much if you don't feel like a "star." Everyone is special in God's eyes. First things first: believe, tell others, get growing. Then see where Christ takes you.

WEEK FIVE

Week Five: SUNDAY

God: Knowing Everything

Take a Look: Psalm 139

> *O LORD, you have searched me and you know me.*
> *Psalm 139:1*

When my brother and I were kids, one of our favorite things to do on summer mornings was to watch *Jeopardy* on TV.

Now, this was the old *Jeopardy*, not the glitzy high-tech version that's on today. The game show set was small, flimsy, and cheap. There wasn't a big electronic game board made of TV monitors; the old one was made of painted wood, with windows that were opened manually by some guy from behind (I wonder what *he's* doing these days). The questions were a lot harder, and the prize money was a lot less impressive. But it was still pretty exciting.

We were especially fascinated one week by a lady contestant named Resa, who was one of the biggest brains ever to appear on the show. Her range of knowledge was awesome. She was coming up with answers (phrased in the form of questions, of course) right and left, blowing away her competition and winning big money. Monday . . . Tuesday . . . Wednesday . . . Thursday . . . Day after day she came out on top. Of course, Friday would be the real test: Could Resa win one more time, becoming *Jeopardy*'s eighth five-day undefeated contestant and qualifying for the prestigious Tournament of Champions later in the year? *Could she?*

Well, the answer was no. On Friday Resa choked. Maybe the question categories didn't match her knowledge as well. Maybe she finally had some decent competition. Maybe she just couldn't handle the pressure. But she finished a disappointing third place that day.

You see, even a really, really smart person can't know everything. When we say that God is all-knowing, or *omniscient*, we're pointing out an important difference between God and human beings. Humans build their knowledge from the bottom up; when we're born, we're a blank slate, and then we slowly start to learn about our world. We hope to keep learning—writing knowledge on that slate—our entire lives. God, on the other hand, possesses knowledge from the top down. He knows all things because he created all things. The *universe* was a blank slate, and from his own mind God filled in all the details as he created them. That's what David is praising in Psalm 139. God's knowledge is shown in his creation.

There are two really important things to scribble on your slate about this.

First, a comforting thought: Because God knows everything, he knows what you need. He knows your problems, your faults, your talents, and your desires—just as he knew David's. You're not alone in life; God sees your every move.

Second, a general rule to live by: The person who knows the most gets to be the teacher. Makes sense, doesn't it? Why grope your way through life? God knows the way. Make him your teacher and guide.

Hey, just thought of something. If God ever went on *Jeopardy*, he could really clean up!

Week Five: MONDAY

Gone Fishing

Take a Look: Matthew 5:13–16

"Come, follow me . . . and I will make you fishers of men."

Matthew 4:19

My brother Tim and I were sitting on a bench in front of the variety store in downtown Grantsburg, Wisconsin, one day—probably eating licorice. It was vacation time up at the cabin, and we were in town with our folks.

So there we were, minding our own business, when an old guy with three days' worth of stubble on his face staggered out of the Rendezvous Bar and decided to strike up a conversation. He came up close—with orange teeth and the kind of breath you wouldn't want near an open flame—looked us in the eye, and said, "Don't sit there—go fishing!"

We stared at him, dumbfounded.

"Don't sit there—go fishing!" he repeated with a look of disgust on his face. Apparently, he thought we ought to grab spin rods and head for the lake.

My brother and I cast sidelong glances at each other, wondering if we should make a run for it.

The old codger smiled, and we realized he was just having some fun. "Don't sit there—go fishing!" He cackled and started to rasp and cough up who knows what as he hobbled off down the street. My brother and I breathed a sigh of relief.

That experience has stayed with me for two reasons: First, that guy was loony tunes. And second, why fishing? Why was fishing the only possible alternative to sitting on a street bench, eating licorice? Was it our civic duty? Was there a town ordinance or something?

When it comes to witnessing for the faith, a lot of Christians are like the pumpkin-toothed man staggering out of the Rendezvous. You can tell they take Christ's commission to be fishers of men quite seriously. To them, witnessing is an opportunity to sink their hooks into someone. So they go out and grab people by the buttonhole or the lapel and make them sit through a gospel presentation. And if you aren't out doing that at every opportunity, what good are you? Don't sit there—go fishing!

I'm not saying that one-on-one street evangelism isn't a useful tool. But there's no way we can use it as our exclusive method of telling people about Christ.

Christ himself balances this view by giving us another one. He says, "You're the light of the world. Let your light shine in a way that allows other people to see your good works and glorify your heavenly Father." In other words, live in a way that makes God look good! Do good things, help people out, feed the hungry, clothe the poor, and eventually people will take notice and say, "Wow, this Christianity must be great stuff if it makes people brand-new like this."

Do you know that statistically, most people become Christians not because of some words somebody threw at them but because they met a Christian who cared, lived honestly, or had a solid marriage?

Maybe you're nervous about admitting you're a Christian—that you have beliefs and convictions different from most of the world. Well, instead of arguing for Christianity, try living it, as Christ suggests. Then see how many "fish" you catch!

Week Five: TUESDAY

You Can't Take It with You

Take a Look: Matthew 6:19–24

> *"Where your treasure is, there your heart will be also."*
> *Matthew 6:21*

Humans are born collectors. Maybe you have a collection, say, of baseball cards. Or dolls. Or butterflies. Or stamps.

There's an interesting story about stamp collectors. Years ago the great aviator Charles Lindbergh had a favorite biplane, named *Jenny*. The U.S. Postal Service decided to immortalize the plane on a postage stamp. Then things got a little crazy.

Due to a printer's error, one hundred of the *Jenny* stamps were printed with the airplane inverted, or upside down. These one hundred stamps became some of the most valuable in the world. But collectors sure had trouble hanging on to them.

Thefts of *Jenny* inverts occurred in New York and Ireland, leading to huge police investigations and the collapse of one of the world's largest stamp auction houses.

Someone started rumors that forty-three of the stamps had gone down on a millionaire's sunken yacht, leading collectors to believe that prices would skyrocket.

One *Jenny* was caught in an air raid during the Battle of Britain in World War II but miraculously survived.

A stamp dealer in Wilkes-Barre, Pennsylvania, had to rush to a bank vault to rescue his three inverts from a flood.

And one collector almost took his prized *Jenny* stamp to the grave with him. Searchers finally found the stamp by looking inside the casket and checking the deceased's coat pocket.

Why all this fuss? Well, to collectors the stamp was special, unique. But when all was said and done, the *Jenny* stamp was not much more than a little piece of paper with glue on the back. This was exactly the kind of thing that Jesus was talking about in Matthew 6. Earthly treasures—your car, clothes, boom box, or CD collection, for instance—may be valuable now, but they're also *vulnerable*. We can lose them to thieves, moths, rust, bombs, floods, and death itself.

What does it mean to "store up treasures in heaven"? In Revelation 22:12 Jesus promises, "Behold, I am coming soon! My reward is with me, and I will give to everyone according to what he has done." That means that our good works in this life will pay off in the next. Helping other people, talking about Jesus, praying, encouraging fellow Christians, being honest, and fighting injustice wherever we find it, among other things, will all be rewarded in heaven —in ways so wonderful we can't even imagine. And nothing and nobody can take that reward away.

Cars may end up in the junkyard. Clothes become old-fashioned. Boom boxes break. Most music is forgotten. But doing good works never goes out of style. And Jesus is keeping a running total of yours. Of course, Jesus loves you, no matter what. But he wants to give you a big reward for working for him. Look at it this way: the most valuable stamp in the world is his stamp of approval.

Sit for a while and think about what you really treasure.

Week Five: WEDNESDAY

Don't Be a Hypocrite

Take a Look: Matthew 23:1–28

> *"First clean the inside of the cup . . . and then the outside also will be clean."*
>
> *Matthew 23:26*

Every January 1, a lot of us take advantage of the fresh start the New Year offers and make some resolutions. We promise to study harder, work harder, lose weight, be on time, and stop biting our nails.

Of course, most of us have a hard time keeping those resolutions, because we go overboard. We make the mistake of choosing goals that require actual effort—a sure formula for failure. So next January 1, don't fall into that trap.

Instead, start the year with a few smaller, easier-to-reach goals. It'll really make you feel good about yourself.

For example: "I know I have a problem submitting to authority, which I need to work on. I resolve that I will not disobey the law of gravity this year." See? Much more realistic than saying you'll obey your curfew.

Try this one: "I want to be more patient this year. So I'll try not to be sixteen until my sixteenth birthday."

Catching on? The key is setting your sights so low, you can't *not* follow through.

Here's another beauty: "No doubt about it, I need to lose some weight. I resolve to take off twenty-five pounds between January 1 and July 1."

This may sound hard at first, but it'll work if you live in a northern climate. When you weigh yourself on January 1, just wear what you normally would that time of year—a heavy parka, winter hiking boots, two sweaters, three pairs of socks—and carry a Coleman stove to keep warm. When you weigh yourself on July 1, wear summer attire—a swimsuit. You may surprise yourself by exceeding your goal. Have a banana split to celebrate!

All kidding aside, if you're willing to settle for the *illusion* of discipline, growth, and accomplishment, this New Year's approach is for you!

Illusion. That's about as much spiritual growth as a lot of people can muster. It was true of the Pharisees, the spiritual leaders of Jesus' day. They put on a good "holy" act, but inside they were just as selfish, ambitious, and phony as anybody else. Maybe more so. These New Year's resolutions were made for them; they liked to bend the rules to suit themselves.

This ticked off Jesus no end. He hated their hypocrisy and told them so. He referred to them as whitewashed tombs and dirty cups—clean on the outside, foul on the inside. You may know some Christians like this—people who talk one way and live another. Sometimes these folks are referred to as "carnal Christians." But putting it more bluntly, they're hypocrites.

What do we do about the hypocrites among us? Well, the truth is, we aren't supposed to judge. We're all hypocritical at times, even if we think we believe all the right things. The best thing we can do about hypocrites is to resolve not to be one of them. Keeping in touch with God and his Word will help us to be sincere, teachable, and usable.

Pray now and ask God for the strength to walk the walk, not just talk the talk.

Week Five: THURSDAY

The Best Gift

Take a Look: Mark 12:28–44

> *"It is more blessed to give than to receive."*
> *Acts 20:35*

It wasn't the most expensive gift—about forty cents, if I remember right—but I'll never forget giving it, because it marked a change in me.

I was about eight years old, and for the first time, I was actually allowed to go Christmas shopping by myself. It was a challenge. I had only a few dollars to spend on my whole family, so I was on a tight budget.

My only sister, Jan, five years older than I, was the hardest to buy for. What did *I* know about what girls liked? But a lady in a small, mom-and-pop gift shop came to my rescue. She pointed me to some little china ring boxes. One was squarish, one was round, one was heart shaped. I picked up one of the boxes. *Something to put her jewelry in,* I mused. It hadn't occurred to me to give her something . . . personal. I was giving everybody else ballpoint pens and stuff.

Questions popped into my mind: Did she already have one of these? What color would she like? What shape? I began to imagine how she would react when she unwrapped it. Would she say, "Ooh! Ah!"? Or just, "Oh"?

I lifted the little lid and took out the wad of white tissue paper inside. Just checking for any special features, I suppose. I liked it. Now, which one to buy? The heart-shaped one? Nah, too Valentine-ish. The square one? The round one? I picked them both up for further scrutiny. Why was this so hard?

I decided on the square ring box with the little painted flowers and had it nicely wrapped. On Christmas Eve, when we opened our presents, Jan seemed pleased—and a little surprised—by my choice.

I can see that box in my mind as if I bought it yesterday. Why? Maybe because for the first time, giving was an investment for me. It was a decision made "outside myself," inspired by the needs and desires of someone else. The eight-year-old-boy sweat I went through, the careful choosing, the desire to please—those were the real gifts I gave my sister that Christmas.

The story of the poor widow in Mark 12 is something like this. For the rich people dropping their bags of money into the temple treasury, giving had become routine. The amounts they were giving out of their surplus wealth, they'd barely miss. But that widow with the two coins—now there's a gift she had to think about. She knew that once she dropped those two coins in the box, she'd be broke for a while. But she did it anyway. She wanted to. She cared.

The point of the story is that giving to God, the church, and other people has to cost us something, or it isn't really giving.

There are lots of things you can give to make someone else's life better—your money, your time, your abilities. But the best gift you can give is the one you sweat for.

Week Five: FRIDAY

The Outsiders

Take a Look: Luke 6:20–28

> *"Love your enemies."*
>
> *Luke 6:27*

I changed high schools in the middle of my junior year. If you've never done it, changing schools midyear can be like trying to stand on a crowded, moving bus: it's the jerks that get you. And I found plenty of those at my new school.

They were everywhere—people who just wouldn't leave the new kid alone. They went out of their way to ridicule me, humiliate me, exclude me. It was bad enough to be new, but being a Christian on top of it didn't make things any easier. It seemed the environment was hostile to that sort of thing.

But eventually I met other Christians at school. They seemed a bit scared, defensive. I don't remember them talking about their faith much—but they were there. Outsiders, like I was, trying their best to "act Christian."

Maybe you've felt like an outsider at school. You face peer pressure, cliques, unsympathetic non-Christians—and with that kind of tension, living like a Christian at school can seem like a tiresome and thankless job.

Jesus knew this would happen. He knew that sending out a bunch of his sheep to live in a world of hungry wolves could mean trouble. Still, we're supposed to be "the salt of the earth" and "the light of the world"—we're supposed to show the way to the truth.

Not everyone will like the truth or will like *us* for pointing it out. But Christ encourages us: "Blessed are you when men hate you, when they exclude you and insult you and reject your name as evil, because of the Son of Man. Rejoice in that day and leap for joy, because great is your reward in heaven. For that is how their fathers treated the prophets" (Luke 6:22–23).

In other words, if you're being rejected because you're a Christian, take heart—you *may* be doing something right. That is, if you're also following Christ's other instructions: "Love your enemies, do good to those who hate you, bless those who curse you, pray for those who mistreat you. . . . Do to others as you would have them do to you" (vv. 27–28, 31). So if you're just being a self-righteous pain in the neck to non-Christians, don't expect a lot of eternal reward.

Your school may sometimes be a negative place, but you can have a positive impact by trying to overcome evil with good.

Week Five: SATURDAY

God Can Use Anybody, Revisited: Judas, Son of James

Take a Look: John 14:15–26

> *"If anyone loves me, he will obey my teaching. My Father will love him, and we will come to him and make our home with him."*
>
> *John 14:23*

When I was in junior high, I got a report card that floored me. My grades were much lower than I had expected. I had pulled a D in one of my best subjects. I panicked. What had happened? Then I glanced at the name at the top. Where it should have said, "Johnson, Thomas E.," it said, "Johnson, Thomas C."

I had received somebody else's report card.

Ever get mixed up with somebody else? It can be unnerving. You can be held responsible for things you haven't done and not get the credit for things you have.

That must have been the burden carried by Judas, son of James. This was *not* Judas Iscariot, the disciple who betrayed Jesus. But after Jesus was crucified, *Judas* became one of the most hated names in the world. You have to wonder if this other Judas took a lot of grief for just having that name.

We don't know much about his later life. But Judas, son of James, helped to clarify a very important truth—a truth that went right to the heart of God's plan of salvation for the world.

The scene: the Last Supper. Jesus is talking with his apostles for the last time before going to the cross. In John 14:15–26 he promises to reveal himself to the disciples in a special way—through the Holy Spirit.

Judas, son of James, pipes up. "But, Lord, why do you intend to show yourself to us and not to the world?" (v. 22).

Good question. At that point, Jesus was very popular with the masses. His triumphal entry into Jerusalem, on the back of a donkey, had been great public relations. He was in a perfect position to take his rightful place as Israel's Messiah and King. Why not reveal himself to the whole world right now?

But God had other plans. Jesus would die for the sins of the world. Then it would be up to the apostles and the church, with the help of the Holy Spirit, to show the world who Christ was. Peter explained this in a sermon he preached at the city of Joppa (Acts 10:38–43).

This should make every Christian feel special. We really do have something the world doesn't have: a living, loving relationship with God—Father, Son, and Holy Spirit—

which gives us the strength and sensitivity to reach out to the world with his message.

So we have Judas, son of James—the obscure guy with the awful name—to thank for making it clear. It was God's plan from the beginning to use people who love him to be his messengers.

The message is love. Pass it on.

WEEK SIX

Week Six: SUNDAY

God: Grace

Take a Look: Ephesians 2:1–10

*For it is by grace you have been saved, through faith—
and this not from yourselves, it is the gift of God—not
by works, so that no one can boast.*

Ephesians 2:8–9

The only subject I really hated in school was math. To
me it was like mental kryptonite.

One reason was the "story" problem. You know, something like this: "Bob and Sue are out on the lake in an aluminum rowboat, 1/4 mile from shore. Suddenly the boat
springs a leak and takes on water at the rate of 135 gallons per
hour. Sue finds a 1 1/2–quart pail and starts bailing at the rate
of 16 pails per minute as Bob starts rowing at a speed of 1 mile
per hour. Halfway to shore, a storm breaks, dumping rain at
a rate of 2 inches per hour and cutting Bob's rowing speed in
half. Question: if the rowboat displaces 350 cubic feet, can Bob
and Sue reach shore before the boat is completely sunk?"

My answer: What kind of a bonehead takes his girlfriend out in an aluminum rowboat when it looks like rain?

My math allergy reached crisis proportions when I
changed schools in the middle of my junior year. My new
math class was deep into a textbook I had never seen, and
was studying material I had no background for. And the
course was set up for independent study, meaning you
worked "at your own pace." Right. My pace in math roughly
matched the continental drift.

My math teacher, Mrs. Jameson, understood my problem. "Just do what you can," she said. "Talk to me when you
have questions. We'll get through this."

So I worked at it, and it got a little easier. But by the last week of the semester, I realized there was no way I'd ever finish. I went to Mrs. Jameson to plead for an extension.

But when I made my pitch, she shook her head. "We couldn't expect you to come in on the middle of this and get it all done," she said. "You lived up to your end of the deal. You made an effort and did what you could. That's all I asked. You've finished the course."

I was stunned and relieved. Of course, I didn't deserve it. Mrs. Jameson could have made me fulfill every last requirement. But she understood my predicament and made a deal with me. In a sense, I had passed that class the day I arrived. She didn't give me justice; she gave me a truckload of mercy.

Sometimes I forget that God has also made a deal—a new covenant—with me. He graciously says, "There's no way you can satisfy all my requirements, so I've sent my Son to save you. Now do what you can. Come to me when you have problems. We'll get through this together." It's what Paul says about God's grace in Ephesians 2: He gives us good things we don't deserve—especially eternal life.

The Christian life is the ultimate independent study course, tailored especially for me. If I check in with the Teacher regularly, I'll make progress in the hard course work of becoming the complete human being he wants me to be, at a pace that's right for me. The best part is that under God's gracious covenant, I've already passed.

Week Six: MONDAY

Here Comes the Judge

Take a Look: Luke 6:35–37

> *"Do not judge, or you too will be judged."*
> *Matthew 7:1*

When I changed schools, I had to adjust to a new reality. For the first time in my life, most of my friends were non-Christians. Many of them smoked, drank, used bad language, and weren't exactly naive sexually. I was a known Christian among unbelievers. How was I supposed to act?

I decided it was my job to show these sinners that Christians were different. I explained to them why I didn't "smoke, drink, swear, chew, or go with girls who do." And I think they respected me for my convictions.

Unfortunately, I wasn't content with just living my convictions. Instead, I became a kind of moral policeman, pointing out the sins of my friends and hoping to influence their behavior (especially that of Liz Ulasawicz—a girl I had a crush on and wanted to convert. I grabbed a cigarette out of Liz's mouth once). I'd call attention to their use of profanity. I always frowned disapprovingly when we had a party and someone brought out something a little stronger than 7-Up. And if they offered *me* any forbidden substances, I self-righteously declined, hoping to illustrate yet another wonderful way in which Christians were "different."

Of course, I thought I was having a really positive impact on my world. No doubt, as a result of my witness, my pagan friends would be turning to Christ in droves.

I found out differently on the opening night of our school play. All of us in the cast and crew were gathering in an offstage room about thirty minutes before curtain time. Liz came in, disgusted about something, and swore. I, of course, felt obligated to call her on it.

Apparently, Liz had had enough. She looked me coldly in the eye and said, loudly enough for everyone to hear, *"Get off my back!"* To my total embarrassment, the entire cast applauded.

I didn't realize how predictable and tedious my behavior had become. Like the Pharisees of Jesus' day, I had taken upon myself the job of judging other people's conduct. And everyone around me had become really tired of it.

Of course, I still didn't approve of all their actions. But it was foolish of me to expect non-Christians to take on values that didn't make sense to them. By trying to make them "act like Christians" before they even knew Christ, I was alienating the very people I was trying to reach.

Instead of judging, my job as a Christian was to love my unsaved friends—to get *off* their backs and *by* their side—to talk to them, listen to them, care about them. I needed to show them the affection and concern that Jesus was so famous for, without compromising my own principles.

It's a lesson I'm still learning. It's easy to judge. It's a lot harder to love.

Week Six: TUESDAY

In Control

Take a Look: Luke 15:11–32

> *"The fear of the LORD is the beginning of wisdom."*
> *Proverbs 9:10*

A Christian youth magazine asked its readers to respond to this question: What are you most looking forward to about being an adult? Why?

The magazine received letters from readers, giving such answers as: "Having a real job," "Being independent," and "Making my own decisions." Most of the responses seemed to have one thing in common: control.

You probably feel the same way about control. You want it. And the prospect of adulthood gives you the hope of someday getting out from under your parents' thumbs. You'll be the boss—chief, kingpin, top dog, head honcho, big cheese, grand pooh-bah—of your life.

Well, it's good to anticipate adulthood, and it's important to keep dreaming and planning for the time when you're on your own. But while you're dreaming, try to keep one thought in mind: being an adult doesn't necessarily make things *easier* for you. There are too many responsibilities to call it "easy," but it can make things *better*—if you're ready for it.

See, there's a big difference between merely being an adult and actually growing up. Anybody over eighteen can be considered an adult, but *growing up* has less to do with age than with what's happening inside you—your attitudes, your values, your goals.

The parable of the prodigal son has a couple of interpretations. Some say it's mainly about the fact that God doesn't play favorites when it comes to salvation. Others say it's about God as a loving Father. Both of these are true. But one thing that can't be argued is the true-to-life nature of the parable itself. This story has been played out a million times. A young man gets itchy, restless, wants to be in control. So he takes control and he blows it—loses his money, his opportunities, his self-respect.

The Prodigal Son didn't realize something really basic: we're never fully in control of our lives. There's always someone to answer to—the law, employers, God. For a Christian, the whole point of growing up and being free to make your own decisions is to work within the rules to do something positive.

So start now. Don't just watch the clock, counting down the hours until you'll be free. Now's the time to get ready—*really* ready.

Week Six: WEDNESDAY

Too Rich?

Take a Look: Luke 18:18–32

"It is easier for a camel to go through the eye of a needle than for a rich man to enter the kingdom of God."
                                                    Luke 18:25

A few years back, the Hamilton Equestrian Center in South Hamilton, Massachusetts, started a new trend in riding stables. It became the first horse condominium development. That's right—horse condos. For just $65,000, owners get a deed to a twelve-foot-by-twelve-foot stall and access to deluxe facilities such as heated riding arenas, outdoor riding rings, a private clubhouse, and several fully equipped tack rooms for riders to store their saddles and gear. Owners pay another $500 a month for maintenance and staff at the center.

When I first read about this concept in a sports magazine, I couldn't help wincing a little. It bugged me that some horses—living in their own $65,000 condominiums—had it better than a lot of people.

Now, I'm all for horses, even though we don't get along. A horse took me on a very scratchy ride through a grove of mulberry trees once, and I've never forgiven her. So maybe I'm not totally objective on this one. But it just seems that people who spend $65,000 on a horse stall have a little more money than they really know what to do with.

In my community, $65,000 buys a respectable two-bedroom home or a four-year college education for two students. Overseas, a children's mission could use $65,000 to provide food, medical treatment, and education for 270 kids for one year—or 27 kids for ten years.

I guess it's all a matter of priorities—what's most important. And that's what Jesus was getting at with the rich young ruler. Here was a guy who seemed to have every-thing—youth, money, social status, power. He had even been faithful to God's Law since he was a kid. But he wanted assurance of eternal life, and he was devastated when Jesus told him to sell everything he had and give the money to the poor. Jesus knew that the young man was hanging on to his wealth and position as a security blanket. The rich young ruler loved his money more than he loved God.

People heavily involved in evangelism tell me that rich, comfortable people are often the hardest to reach with the gospel. Why? Because they feel they can take care of them-selves; they don't think they need Jesus. And that often blinds them to other people's needs, too. Self-sacrifice and total dependence on God make up that narrow eye of the needle they have so much trouble squeezing through. Amer-icans are better off financially than most people in the world. So American Christians have a special responsibility. Even though we're already saved, we need to check our hearts once in a while and make sure we're willing to spend a little less on ourselves and more on people who don't have as much as we do. We need to ask ourselves: *Do we love our money more than we love God?*

Week Six: THURSDAY

Living Water

Take a Look: John 4:7–14

> "*Whoever drinks the water I give him will never thirst.*"
>
> *John 4:14*

I've owned a lot of wristwatches in my life, and one thing I've found is that some watches labeled "water resistant" promise more than they deliver. Wear them into the pool or subject them to a wash and spin in the old Maytag, and you're off to the drugstore for a new Timex.

Now a Texas company has invented a new kind of watch, one that *needs* a swim once in a while. The watch runs on batteries, made of zinc and copper, that require liquid to function. So instead of winding it or changing the battery, you just give it a bath. And any liquid will do—water, Coke, milk, grapefruit juice—anything you have handy.

Water that energizes. That's not a bad way to look at the analogy Jesus made about the love-and-faith relationship we can have with him. The Samaritan woman at the well, in John 4, didn't quite get it, but Jesus was using an image mentioned all through the Bible—"water of life," "living water," being "planted by streams of water," "a cup of cold water." Water was very important to the people of the arid Middle East in Jesus' time, as it is today. And of course, it's important to us too. On a hot day, a cold glass of water quenches your thirst, cools you down, picks you up. It's what you *need*.

That's what the experience of Christ's love and forgiveness can do for you. It's a great relief, but it also gives you the spiritual energy you need to go on. Once you know you're loved and forgiven, your old sins don't hold you back. Life is brighter, more purposeful. The things you do at school, at work, and at church have more meaning, because you're building your spiritual future. You're a regular Energizer Bunny—you have energy to keep going, because life is worth living.

So if this living water is so great, why don't some Christians seem more full of life? Why do they seem so dried up? Maybe it's because they've forgotten that God really has forgiven them and loves them. That's why daily devotions are so important. They remind us that we have

a real relationship with Christ and that we have this relationship because of God's love and forgiveness.

Living water is yours for the asking. Drink up!

Week Six: FRIDAY

The Real Thing?

Take a Look: John 6:53–71

> *"The words I have spoken to you are spirit and they
> are life. Yet there are some of you who do not believe."*
> John 6:63–64

Back in 1985 the Coca-Cola Company goofed. They
introduced New Coke (which, to my taste, was just a clone
of Pepsi), discarding the much loved traditional Coke
formula.

Everybody screamed. OK, not *everybody*, but so many
people made a fuss about bringing back the old Coke that
the company came up with Coca-Cola Classic. So everybody should have been satisfied, right?

Not quite. Some consumers insisted that Coke Classic
tasted "different" from the old Coke. They couldn't put
their finger on it, but something wasn't right. Were they just
imagining things? Nope. It turns out that while the old *formula* came back, different sweeteners were used in Classic.
Instead of sucrose (from sugarcane and beets), bottlers
started using fructose and glucose (from corn). Scientists who
tested both Cokes claimed that there really was a difference
in taste.

The difference was subtle, hard to detect. But the pros
could tell. It's like what Jesus was doing in John 6. He was
using his superior powers to detect which of his followers

"tasted" different—who was a phony and who was "the real thing."

Last week we talked about hypocrites, Christians who say one thing and do another. Here we're looking at people who followed Jesus but who never really believed in him. They were part of the herd but not part of his flock. Get it?

Why would people do that? Why would they tag along with someone they didn't really believe in? Well, there was a lot of curiosity about Jesus. He was new, different. People wanted to catch the latest wave. But for many Jesus was just a fad. When Jesus confronted them with the truth, they dropped out.

There are people like this in churches. They show up every Sunday, pretending. Maybe because church life is a good social outlet or just because it makes them feel better. The same may be true for your youth group. You may even sense who some of these kids are. But how should you relate to them?

Some youth groups are so separated, so closed, they wouldn't know what to do with a non-Christian if one showed up. But when an unbeliever visits your group, see that person as an *opportunity*. A pastor I once talked to knew that a lot of the people who attended his church were phonies. But he said, "I'm just thankful we can get these people here and preach the gospel to 'em. Some of them will eventually be reached."

That's how you can look at the marginal kids in your group. Christian stuff is happening all around them, but they may not be "getting it." By being a friend, talking to them, and living your faith, you can help them begin to catch on. Eventually you might even be able to get pretty specific about where they are spiritually.

Remember: although Jesus was disappointed in those phony sheep of his, he *wanted* them to believe, to get real. Make that your desire, too.

Week Six: SATURDAY

God Can Use Anybody, Part VI: Bartholomew (Nathanael)

Take a Look: John 1:45–51

> *"Nazareth! Can anything good come from there?"*
> *Nathanael asked.*
> *"Come and see," said Philip.*
>
> *John 1:46*

There's a bit of confusion about the identity of today's apostle. In the gospels of Matthew, Mark, and Luke, Bartholomew and Philip are always mentioned together. But when we get to John's gospel, Philip is hanging out with a guy named Nathanael, and Bartholomew isn't even mentioned. So most Bible scholars assume that Bartholomew and Nathanael are the same person. It's a pretty safe bet.

But whichever name you call him by, Bartholomew-Nathanael is best known for one thing: before meeting Jesus, he was a snob.

When Philip excitedly told Nathanael that he had found Jesus of Nazareth, the Messiah, Nathanael wrinkled his nose and said, "Can anything good come from there?" Apparently, Nazareth had a bad reputation at the time. Nathanael assumed that anybody who came from a scuzzy town had to be a scuzzy person.

Have you ever fallen into that trap? My high school friends and I did. The rivalry between schools in my city was intense, especially in athletics. When we'd go to basketball games, we'd see the opposing team and their fans as a cut below our team, our school . . . *us*. If we lost a game to them, it was a matter of lousy refing or plain old bad luck. We just *knew* that the kids from Lincoln High were lower class or that Southeast High kids were spoiled, rich brats or that East High kids were spoiled, newly rich brats or that kids from Pius X went to a little class-B parochial school and we'd always be able to mop the basketball court with 'em.

Of course, all those other kids saw my school, Northeast High, as a place where the guys drank a lot and the girls got pregnant a lot (those impressions were sort of accurate, unfortunately). The point is, none of these stereotypes was entirely fair. But to feel better about ourselves, we created a negative image of others.

That's what Bartholomew-Nathanael was doing. He had an image of Nazareth—and Nazarenes—in mind, and it influenced his thinking about Jesus. Still, he did have a quality that some of us don't—he was willing to be proved *wrong*. When he met Jesus, he was won over right away. He could see that Jesus was someone special. He changed his mind.

How about you? Are you willing to have your own stereotypes proved wrong? It's good to remember that most people your age don't have any control over where they live or go to school and that they definitely can't pick who their parents are or whether they're rich, poor, or somewhere in the middle. They're taking life as it's been dished out to them and simply want to be given a chance—just like you.

Pray and ask God for the grace to meet people open-mindedly.

WEEK
SEVEN

Week Seven: SUNDAY

God: Spirit

Take a Look: Romans 8:1–17

Those who are led by the Spirit of God are sons of God.
Romans 8:14

Stephen Hawking is one of the smartest people in the world. In fact, people who know say that he's the most brilliant theoretical physicist since Albert Einstein. He has written books, won awards, and is highly respected in his field.

But he has done most of this from a wheelchair. When he was twenty-one and still a college student, he was diagnosed with amyotrophic lateral sclerosis—Lou Gehrig's disease—which disables nerves and muscles. He is now unable to move his limbs, write for himself, or speak understandably, except to those who know him very well. All of his work is done in his head, then slowly dictated to a secretary.

There he is—one of the greatest minds of the twentieth century—imprisoned in a body that no longer works. It makes you wonder what he could accomplish if he were healthy. Stephen Hawking is a victim of what happens to flesh-and-blood bodies: they get corrupted, fail, and wear out. And eventually they turn to dust.

God doesn't have those limitations. He doesn't have a corruptible physical body; he is spirit, and that means he is eternal and free. He can come and go as he pleases. He is not bound by gravity, the atmosphere, or time—he *created* all those things. Being a spirit is one of the things that makes him God and makes him able to do what he does.

It's hard for me to grasp this spirit thing. When I think of spirit, I think of . . . thin air. But even air is made up of molecules, matter. Still, spirit isn't *nothing;* it's *something* we can't see or measure. That's where faith comes in; it's knowing and believing in someone I can't see, but trust anyway.

We know from the Bible that God exists as three persons: Father, Son, and Holy Spirit. (As a reminder, check out the story of Jesus' baptism, in Mark 1:9–11—the Father, Son, and Spirit are all there.) They're all God, all equal, and all one. But each person has his own work to do. Roughly speaking—*very* roughly—the Father creates us, the Son saves us, and the Holy Spirit lives in us.

This is where God really becomes visible—in the work of the Holy Spirit. Something happens to us when we accept Christ; the Holy Spirit comes inside—prompting us, reminding us, guiding us, teaching us. We have a choice about how much control we give over to the Holy Spirit in our lives. But the more we do, the more we grow. That's what Paul is saying in Romans 8: we can be enslaved by our old sinful nature, or we can respond to the Spirit and become the whole people we were meant to be.

The Holy Spirit is like a seed planted in our hearts, a seed that sprouts and bears the fruit of good works and good attitudes. That fruit is an I.D. card that proves we belong to Christ. We'll take a look at our Christian I.D. over the next two weeks.

Meanwhile, remember: the Holy Spirit is working to make you better—from the *inside.*

Week Seven: MONDAY

Christian I.D.: Love, Part One

Take a Look: 1 Corinthians 13

> *The greatest of these is love.*
> *1 Corinthians 13:13*

The fruit of the Spirit is love.
Galatians 5:22

In the fall of my senior year, I was on the staff of my high school newspaper. That's where I met Liz.

Liz was our feature editor and everything I wanted in a girl. She was beautiful. But it wasn't only her looks that attracted me. She was smart, talented, had a great sense of humor (translation: she laughed at my jokes), and her rich parents didn't hurt, either. I wanted to date her almost as much as I'd wanted that red bike back in fourth grade.

There was one hitch—she wasn't a Christian. But I figured I could fix that. I could also take care of her on-and-off boyfriend, Bill. With my vast reserves of charm and sensitivity, I'd woo her, win her, convert her to Christ, and make her forget old Bill. It was quite a project I had planned. Liz would be mine.

But things didn't work out as I had hoped. Liz and I were friends, but we couldn't seem to get together. We *almost* went out about four times; the plans always fell through. I invited her to church, and that didn't pan out, either. But I still hoped and hoped and hoped—all the way up to graduation, at which time Liz and I wished each other the best and never saw each other again.

I've thought about Liz often since then, most of the time with embarrassment. The truth is, I wasn't ready for a dating relationship with Liz or anyone else. I was so caught up in my romantic fantasies and schemes that I hadn't learned the basics of relating to girls in a sincere way, letting them know the real me. For me Liz wasn't even a real person, with her own needs and desires. She was a dream, a status symbol—just like that red bike back in fourth grade. Did I really like her or just what she could do for my ego?

In 1 Corinthians 13 Paul says, "Love is patient, love is kind. It does not envy, it does not boast, it is not proud. It is not rude, it is not self-seeking" (vv. 4–5). What I needed with Liz was the patience to let our friendship develop naturally, and not grab for her affection; the kindness to value her interests, not just my own; and the humility to forget about being jealous of Bill or desiring a "trophy" I could brag about.

In relationships, caring and companionship are what count the most. Not money, good looks, or glamour. Not owning somebody, as you would a boom box or a new set of radial tires. Just unselfish interest and mutual respect.

More tomorrow. Until then, try an experiment: Go out and find somebody to love—really love, in the way 1 Corinthians 13 describes it. Avoid making love a game with a prize you have to win at all costs, and you'll find out how natural and relaxed and fun it can be for both of you.

Week Seven: TUESDAY

Christian I.D.: Love, Part Two

Take a Look: 1 John 4:7–21

> *A friend loves at all times.*
> *Proverbs 17:17*

> *The fruit of the Spirit is love.*
> *Galatians 5:22*

Yesterday I told you about Liz, a girl I met in my junior year of high school. About the same time, I met Gretchen. She liked writing, acting, and music, as I did. And she was a Christian. We hit it off right away.

I'd better tell you, though, that Gretchen was . . . eccentric. Her vocabulary and her mannerisms made her seem more proper and grown-up than your typical teenager. Then as I got to know her better, I found out she had a lot of problems, and she started depending on me for support.

I took this as the beginnings of a romantic interest, so I pulled back a little. I didn't like feeling trapped. And besides, if you'll remember, I had bigger fish to fry with Liz. Oh, boy.

Years after graduation, when we were both working in Chicago, Gretchen called one night and invited me to dinner and a play. I went, but from the very start of the evening, I was uncomfortable. Gretchen seemed even a little more eccentric than usual. We made awkward small talk—until I drove her home. As we sat in my car at the curb, I got an earful.

Her life, she told me, was a mess. She felt lonely, detached. She had taken to a life of sexual promiscuity, walking up to total strangers on subway platforms and inviting them to bed. She had contracted a venereal disease but was getting treatment. Her mother, shocked by this revelation, was no help at all. And God didn't seem to fit in anywhere.

I didn't know what to say. I reeled off some Christian platitudes and clichés but winced inside at every word. I felt powerless to help her, and I know I didn't.

Driving home, I could have kicked myself. It wasn't that I felt responsible for Gretchen's life—she had made her own choices. But what was she looking for on those subway platforms? Not sex, really. I think she was desperately searching for another kind of closeness. She wanted someone to accept her, with all of her talents and eccentricities. What she needed, and what she had needed in high school, was a true friend.

What if I had taken all the energy I'd wasted daydreaming, hoping, and fantasizing about Liz and had pumped it into an honest-to-goodness friendship with Gretchen? Maybe I could have given her what she needed. And maybe I would have learned sooner that it was more important for me to be friends with a girl than to have a girlfriend.

In today's reading, John tells us that as Christians, we're able to act in a loving way, even toward needy and difficult people, because God loved us first. His Spirit of love flows out of us. But it all depends on how willing we are to let the Spirit do his work.

God wants to love people through us. There are a lot of Gretchens out there.

Week Seven: WEDNESDAY

Christian I.D.: Joy

Take a Look: Luke 2:1–38

"Do not be afraid. I bring you good news of great joy."
Luke 2:10

The fruit of the Spirit is . . . joy.
Galatians 5:22

Wasn't it kind of neat to read the Christmas story again? Since it's one of the greatest chapters in the Bible, why save it just for the Christmas season? It's a story of God interacting with real people.

One of the people in this story, old Simeon, reminds me of a man named Les. Les was one of the most positive people I have ever met. He went to my church, and although he was seventy-one years old, his upbeat attitude made him seem years younger.

My father greeted him once in a church hallway, with a casual, "How are ya, Les?"

"Better," Les replied.

My dad stopped and looked at him with concern. "What do you mean—have you been sick?"

"No." Les shrugged. "I'm just *better*." To him every day was better than the one before. He felt good about himself, about life, and about other people. He was optimistic down to his bones. His good nature never seemed to quit.

It was obvious that Les had something good going on inside that let him be such a sunny person on the outside. He had the joy, joy, joy, joy, down in his heart. The kind of joy the angel promised the shepherds in Luke 2.

So what does joy mean? Happiness? Giddiness? Excitement? It can mean all of those things, but it goes deeper. Real joy comes from the confidence that something good is happening or going to happen—that no matter how dark life gets, things will get better, because God doesn't hang his children out to dry.

Simeon was living with the expectation that Israel, a country under the oppressive thumb of the Roman empire, would one day have a Deliverer. And as promised by the Holy Spirit, he lived to see it.

Les was living with the expectation that tomorrow would be better than today, that *he* would be better. He believed that God would never stop working in his life.

What are you expecting in your life? As a Christian, the joy of the Spirit means you can expect something good. That doesn't mean every day will be roses. It doesn't mean you'll be busting a gut with laughter all the time. But it does mean that you can look for the good in every person and situation you meet up with. And that can make a big difference in your relationships. People are drawn to others who have a happy outlook on life.

Sit right now with your eyes closed. Remember the good things God has done for you. Imagine all the ways he'll be there for you in the future. Think about the chance God has given you to change your world for the better. Feel the joy!

Week Seven: THURSDAY

Christian I.D.: Peace

Take a Look: Philippians 3:7–14

> *The fruit of the Spirit is . . . peace.*
> *Galatians 5:22*

Something was wrong, and everybody onstage knew it. The second performance of our eighth-grade play—a Christmas extravaganza complete with a vocal ensemble, a mime troupe, and a concert band, in which I played the lead—was sliding off the rails to disaster.

Things had been going great until the second act. But halfway through the play, I got confused and skipped ahead in the script. And not just a few lines, either—I jumped past *pages and pages* of action and dialogue.

It wouldn't have been so bad if everything had come to a grinding halt. But no, we kept going—the other actors *jumped ahead with me*! Pretty soon the action wasn't making any sense.

The vocal group, which should have been onstage, costumed like Christmas carolers, were nowhere to be found. The mime troupe, which should have been ready for the "shepherds go to the manger" scene, were instead dressed up like Christmas toys. The band was all cued up for the wrong music. It was a mess.

My head was spinning. Somehow we muddled through to an early conclusion. But the sickening fact was, I had blown the play to smithereens, with an audience there to watch. *How would I ever live it down?*

Well, it wasn't as bad as I thought. People were upset with me, but not forever. The other performances went well, and afterward we had a terrific cast party where everybody begged me to perform. I even won a student drama award that year. I had screwed up but people got over it.

A few years ago I ran across my script for the play, yellowed with age. But the memory of my humiliation came back like a new wound, ugly and painful. I relived it all: the panic, the embarrassment, the stupidity of it all. I kicked myself. Why was I such a jerk?

Then it hit me: the only person who hadn't forgiven me was *me*. Here I was, all grown up, beating my head against the wall for something nobody cared about anymore.

I had forgotten the power of God's forgiveness and the help of the Holy Spirit. In a mysterious way, the Spirit makes it possible for a believer to settle the conflicts in his life and make peace—with God, with himself, with others, and with the past.

We can all think of moments in our lives that we regret. But we can move past them. The apostle Paul saw his failings as clearly as anyone. But he was able to put the bad stuff behind him, to keep learning and growing, to "press on," because he knew that God had given him a fresh start. He had peace.

Do you keep pounding yourself because of the past? God has work for you to do. And you'll never get it done if you're torn up inside by old conflicts. Ask the Holy Spirit to help you work them out.

Week Seven: FRIDAY

Christian I.D.: Patience

Take a Look: 1 Thessalonians 5:12–28

> *Be patient with everyone.*
> *1 Thessalonians 5:14*

> *The fruit of the Spirit is . . . patience.*
> *Galatians 5:22*

As I stood in line at the supermarket checkout, quietly waiting my turn, I couldn't help but smolder over the injustice of it all.

The woman ahead of me—an employee of the supermarket, it turned out—was holding things up. First she handed the cashier a big bunch of discount coupons at the last minute. Then when the final total of $46.23 came up on the cash register, the woman discovered she didn't have enough money. So she started giving groceries back, one at a time, while the cashier filled out an "over ring" form for each item until the total went below $40.00.

I looked behind me. People with full shopping carts were lined up all the way back to the freezer cases. All I had to buy was a couple of liters of Diet Coke and a *TV Guide,* but I was stuck in this traffic jam. What was wrong with this woman? Why couldn't she get organized? Why didn't she keep a running total as she shopped, so she'd have enough money at the end? Couldn't she see she was making me wait, making us all wait? Who did she think she was?

Then I caught myself. Maybe I didn't know the whole story. Maybe this woman was down to her last forty bucks and had a houseful of kids to feed. Maybe she was in a hurry, because of some emergency.

I realized that my impatience was really selfishness. I wasn't thinking about this woman's problems, only my own. I just hate to wait, and I get really antsy when I have to—in traffic, at the bank, at a restaurant. I especially hate being held up by people who aren't as fast, or as smart, as I think I am. It's one of my least attractive qualities.

But the fruit of the Spirit is patience. The old King James Version calls it "long-suffering." In other words, it's a matter of how much you can put up with for how long. How does the Spirit teach me patience? By reminding me— as he did in the supermarket checkout line—that I'm not the only person in the world. Other people have problems, needs, and obstacles in their lives, that I know nothing about. When I'm willing to wait for them, I'm cutting them the same kind of slack I want for myself.

In 1 Thessalonians 5 Paul is saying that patience is a key part of a Christian's whole attitude—right along with helping, encouraging, and wanting the best for other people (vv. 14–15). And the Holy Spirit is always there to remind us of that. All we have to do is listen.

Week Seven: SATURDAY

God Can Really Use Anybody: Matthew

Take a Look: Luke 5:27–39

"It is not the healthy who need a doctor, but the sick."
Luke 5:31

When Jesus chose Matthew (also known as Levi) as one of his disciples, he didn't just pick somebody with a few personality flaws. He picked someone who was hated by the entire country.

You see, Matthew was a *publican*—that is, a tax collector. Publicans were usually local guys hired by the Roman government, and they were known for charging too much, threatening phony legal action to get hush money, and generally being a pain in the neck. They were, simply, corrupt government officials.

Why would Jesus want a guy like that on his team?

Well, why would Jesus want a guy like Chuck Colson on his team? Over twenty years ago Colson was a government type back in President Nixon's administration. He was the White House "hatchet man," who got back at the president's enemies. He worked so hard at it that he ended up breaking several laws and landing in jail.

But in the middle of his troubles, Colson found Christ. His life changed dramatically, and now he's the head of a Christian ministry to people behind bars. It took a long time for some people to believe that Chuck Colson's conversion was sincere. But now he's regarded as one of America's best spokesmen for Christianity.

People were also suspicious of Matthew and his relationship with Jesus. When Matthew threw a big reception for Jesus at his house, a lot of his friends—fellow publicans and other lowlife—were there. The scribes and Pharisees were appalled. They said to Jesus, "How can you hang out with such riffraff?" Jesus' answer is one of my favorite verses, and the best answer you can give to people who criticize you for having non-Christian friends: "It is not the healthy who need a doctor, but the sick" (v. 31). Jesus heals people who are sick with sin.

That's what Christ did for Matthew. Jesus took a man who had victimized hundreds—maybe thousands—of people and made him into a servant. In addition to writing the gospel that has his name on it, Matthew, according to tradition, preached in Judea (the area where he'd done all that bad stuff) for about fifteen years after Jesus' ascension. Then he went as a missionary to other countries. There's nothing like a truly changed life to get people to take a second look at the gospel. It shows the power of God's love and forgiveness.

Have you ever been suspicious of a new believer with an ugly past, or critical of Christians who hang around with these types? Remember, Jesus is the Great Physician; he can heal anybody. And he can use anybody.

WEEK
EIGHT

Week Eight: SUNDAY

God: Righteous

Take a Look: Psalm 97

> *The heavens proclaim his righteousness, and all the*
> *peoples see his glory.*
>
> *Psalm 97:6*

It was a time of great civil war. The Republic, having been ruled in wisdom by the Senate, aided by the Jedi Knights, had been taken over by a corrupt senator who had declared himself emperor. Exiled factions loyal to the old Republic were trying to overthrow the Empire but were threatened by the Empire's secret weapon—the Death Star, a huge space station the size of a small moon, with laser weapons powerful enough to destroy whole star systems. Princess Leia was being held hostage aboard the Death Star, but she got a message to an old Jedi Knight, Obi-wan Kenobi. The Empire and the Death Star had to be stopped, but the job fell to an unlikely hero—a young man named Luke Skywalker. . . .

Sound familiar? There's hardly anyone who's been around for a while who doesn't know the plot of *Star Wars,* George Lucas's intergalactic tale of good and evil. It's one of the most successful movies ever made.

Think about the Death Star for a minute. It was really pretty awesome. It was the product of meticulous planning, a masterpiece of engineering, a technical marvel, the ultimate achievement. But it was also the ultimate threat, because it put absolute power in the wrong hands—the hands of an evil empire bent on crushing everything in its path.

That's why when I think about God, Psalm 97 is such a relief. "The LORD reigns, let the earth be glad," says verse 1. Why? Because "righteousness and justice are the foundation of his throne" (v. 2). If God were powerful and not righteous—like the ruler of the Empire—the universe would be a pretty scary place. And if God were righteous but not powerful, he couldn't do anything for his children.

But because he is both, we can be glad and give thanks (v. 12). God has absolute power, but he always does what's right. That means he can be trusted to do what's best—for us and for the people we care about.

God's righteous power is available to you through prayer and reading his Word. Take some time now to tap into it.

Week Eight: MONDAY

Christian I.D.: Kindness

Take a Look: Colossians 3:5–17

> *Clothe yourselves with compassion.*
> *Colossians 3:12*

> *The fruit of the Spirit is . . . kindness.*
> *Galatians 5:22*

Diane was one of those people you just knew was *going places*. She was editor of my high school newspaper, a top student, a national merit scholar, and involved in *everything*. To me she seemed to have it all together. Then one day we went out for a Coke after school, and when I drove her home, she told me how tough her life really was.

It turned out that her mother had serious problems with depression—in fact, she'd been in a mental hospital for a while. Now that she was back home, there was daily tension. She would sleep in until after noon, and then she would watch TV all day in her pajamas and bathrobe. She didn't keep house, didn't fix dinner, didn't do much of anything except pick fights with the family.

Because she slept so much during the day, Diane's mom couldn't sleep when she went to bed at the normal family bedtime. She would toss and turn for hours, then get up and start screaming at the top of her lungs out of frustration. Then the whole family would have to wake up and deal with her. Every day was the same thing. It looked hopeless.

Diane carried this burden around all the time, and hardly anybody knew. She never talked about it and never had friends over. Outwardly Diane appeared popular, successful, and happy. Inside, she lived in despair. I'm glad she trusted me with her secret. I was able to listen and share Christ with her.

At first she was skeptical of anything religious. "Why should I believe in Christianity any more than Greek mythology?" she asked. But the more we talked, the more she started to see some things. "Hmmm. You may convert me yet," she said once.

I never was able to lead her to a definite commitment, although I did plant some seeds. The point is, I listened to her first.

In today's reading, Paul talks about negative behavior—anger, wrath, malice, slander, and abusive speech. These behaviors are definitely unkind; they hurt people. Then he encourages positive behavior—compassion, kindness, gentleness, forgiveness, love. If we let the Spirit help us with the kind behaviors, the unkind ones will start to take care of themselves. And if we develop a reputation for kindness toward others, people who are hurting—people like Diane—will trust us enough to open up, and we can show the love of Christ to them.

Someone near you is carrying a heavy burden. Be a friend they can share it with.

Week Eight: TUESDAY

Christian I.D.: Goodness

Take a Look: Ephesians 5:1–21

The fruit of the light consists in all goodness, righteousness and truth.

Ephesians 5:9

The fruit of the Spirit is . . . goodness.

Galatians 5:22

Good. Goody-goody. Good guy. Good egg. Goody Two-shoes. Good little boy. Goodness gracious!

Remember back in week 3, when we talked about *holiness* and how the word has really taken a beating? The word *goodness* is in the same boat. Sometimes we think of goodness as only applying to prim schoolteachers with their hair up in a bun, perfect children in little suits and frilly dresses, or faithful dogs who lie around quietly on the floor and don't drink out of the toilet. To be "good" means to stay out of trouble and, for the most part, to stay out of the way. Good people are expected to sit on the sidelines and watch the world go by.

Or are they? In today's Scripture reading, Paul talks plenty about rejecting badness as part of the Christian lifestyle. He cranks out quite a list of bad things that the Ephesians and some of their neighbors had been involved in. Some were so bad, he wouldn't even spell them out. But then, in verses 15–17, he tells the people to be wise and make the most of their time. For what? For getting things done—

good things. For getting closer to God, loving each other, and then showing that love to the rest of their world. Goodness is not just the *absence* of badness but a war *against* badness. It means "Christian service" in the most active sense.

Sometimes our definitions of Christian service can be pretty narrow, with an emphasis on church activities, occasional blitzes of street evangelism, and Christmas caroling at the local nursing home.

Of course, all those things are great. But how about broadening your horizons a bit? There are lots of ways you can wage war against badness and make your community a better place: fighting ignorance and poverty by helping children (and adults) learn to read, taking food to the hungry, spending time with the elderly and others who are neglected, and cleaning up litter and pollution in the environment, to name a few. All of these activities go along with the Christian virtues of love, compassion, and doing good and can be done by individuals or groups. Some people call this kind of involvement *pre-evangelism*. It shows that Christians really do care about making the world a better place and helps the gospel make sense to people.

You can get involved. Talk to a teacher or youth pastor about some ideas and then commit to actually doing something on a continuing basis. It may only take a few hours of your time each week. And while you're out doing good, find ways to let people know you're doing this stuff for a reason: you love others because Jesus first loved you (1 John 4:19).

Week Eight: WEDNESDAY

Christian I.D.: Faithfulness

Take a Look: Luke 12:35–48

> *The fruit of the Spirit is . . . faithfulness.*
> *Galatians 5:22*

There are some firsts in life you never forget: your first date, your first kiss, your first job. And your first car.

Mine was a 1965 Rambler American that I shared with my brother Tim (some firsts aren't perfect). It was pretty weather-beaten—a faded red with rusty fenders. It had no radio, no air conditioning, no carpeting, and the transmission liked to grind between gears. But it was *ours*.

Tim and I started putting the car in shape. We applied finish restorer, patched the rust spots and repainted them (not quite a perfect match), bought some tires, and got a tune-up. We even installed a cheap radio. And you know, the final result wasn't too shabby. That Rambler turned into a pretty good car. We drove it for thousands of miles. Of course, it *was* pretty ugly. Our college friends had a nickname for it—the Box. But when they needed to borrow a car, they didn't seem to mind driving it. It was Old Reliable.

After a few years of sharing a car, Tim decided to buy his own, and I had the Rambler all to myself. By this time, however, the Box was really getting tired. It had starting problems, a bad clutch, bald tires, and returning rust. Getting it in shape wouldn't be cheap. When the Box started leaking antifreeze, I gave up on it. I signed over the title to a local mechanic, who said he would scrap the car for me. I had closed the book on the Box's long, distinguished career.

Or so I thought.

Months later, after I'd bought another car, I was stopped at a red light, when a very familiar-looking Rambler made a left turn in front of me. Sure enough, it was the Box, with its trademark nonmatching paint and everything.

I kicked myself. The mechanic had lied to me! Instead of scrapping the car, he had fixed it up and sold it, no doubt at a nice profit. I felt angry and stupid. I could have saved and owned that car, instead of making payments on the new one. But I had lost my chance.

It was a good lesson: everything that's worth anything is worth taking care of, and I have to keep at it. That's what faithfulness is all about. It means that over the long haul, I can be counted on to do what needs to be done.

In today's reading, Jesus says faithfulness is one of the most important qualities for a believer. In everyday life, it applies to taking care of cars, homes, jobs, relationships, and anything else God entrusts to me—especially my spiritual life. Jesus wants me to do the important, everyday work of faith so he can reward me with even greater trust. If I don't do it, someone else will—and I'll be the loser.

Week Eight: THURSDAY

Christian I.D.: Gentleness

Take a Look: Proverbs 15

> *A gentle answer turns away wrath.*
> *Proverbs 15:1*

> *The fruit of the Spirit is . . . gentleness.*
> *Galatians 5:22–23*

One of the toughest things for a writer is rejection. When you send out a manuscript to a magazine or a book publisher, you have high hopes. You want them to *love* it, say it's the greatest thing they've ever read, and mail you a nice fat check for your efforts. But instead of a check, you often get a preprinted rejection slip, telling you to take your manuscript and get lost (at least, that's what it feels like). Writing is hard enough, but to be told your stuff is no good, in a cold form letter, is like *death*.

When I worked on a magazine staff, we came up with a different kind of letter for rejecting stories and articles. We thanked the writer for the submission, then listed reasons why we felt that the manuscript wasn't for us. Below the list was a space for written comments and suggestions about what was wrong with the piece and what might make it better. The final paragraph wished them the best in their pursuit as a writer.

That letter was based on a good rule that gentle, sensitive people use when dishing out constructive criticism: "Give 'em a *sandwich*." In other words, say something nice, give them the criticism, then wind up with something nice again. Since the bad stuff is sandwiched in between two pieces of good stuff, it's easier to take and easier to put in perspective.

This approach really paid off. I got a lot of letters from writers, thanking me for taking the time to give them some constructive advice instead of just sending a form letter.

Proverbs 15 might seem at first like a hodgepodge of old sayings. But if you look through the whole chapter, you begin to see a running theme of gentleness. Phrases like "gentle answer" (v. 1), "tongue that brings healing" (v. 4), "cheerful heart" (v. 15), "patient man" (v. 18), "apt reply" (v. 23), "weighs its answers" (v. 28), and "good news" (v. 30) all hint at behavior that is not harsh but positive and constructive, making other people feel good. It's amazing how the right, gentle word at the right time, even in a painful situation, can make all the difference.

Next time you feel like criticizing someone, stop and think. Listen to the prompting of the Holy Spirit. Ask yourself: *Do I really need to say this? Is there something I can say along with it to soften the blow? How can I let this person know that I'm not just being critical but that I really care?*

Week Eight: FRIDAY

Christian I.D.: Self-Control

Take a Look: 2 Peter 1:1–11

> *The fruit of the Spirit is . . . self-control.*
> *Galatians 5:22–23*

It seems everybody's got a nickname these days. You've heard of "yuppies." Those initials stand for Young Urban Professionals—people in their twenties and thirties on the way up. Then there are married couples called "dinks" (Double Income, No Kids). And if you're a teenager with a job, you're one of the "skippies."

Skippies?

That's right—School Kids with Income and Purchasing Power. You make money in a variety of ways, and you spend it. Your purchases account for billions of dollars a year in the economy.

Having that money in your pocket can be a great feeling. It means freedom, security, having a little control over your life. The problem with money, though, is that it sometimes controls *us*. We get carried away with the power that money gives us, and before we know it, it's gone.

The truth is, we don't need to learn how to control *money;* we need to learn how to control *ourselves,* and that will affect our success in every part of our lives.

"The fruit of the Spirit is . . . self-control." That doesn't mean you hang limp while God pulls your strings. You're not a puppet; you're a person. Self-control means being aware of what you're doing, cutting out things that are hurting you, making wise choices and sticking to them. The Holy Spirit is always there to remind us of what's right, but he won't do all the work for us. Living for Jesus is a partnership.

So what does self-control mean in real life? It means not eating a whole bag of Doritos at one sitting, because you know you'll feel lousy and your breath will be toxic in the morning. It means making enough time for exercise and rest—even though other activities are a lot more fun—because you know it'll help you to be physically and mentally sharp, especially when you've got exams coming up. It means not pressing your date for more intimate physical contact—even though your hormones are banging on the door—because you know there'll be a better time for that.

And where money is concerned, it means putting yourself on a budget and trying to get the most for your buck, because you know that being broke is the pits.

In today's reading, Peter outlines the steps of Christian maturity: faith, moral excellence, knowledge, self-control, perseverance, godliness, brotherly kindness, and love.

It's no accident that knowledge and self-control are right next to each other, because self-control is a matter of acting on what we know to be true and right. How do we know? By experience. By praying and reading the Bible. By learning from the advice and discipline of our folks. And by the Spirit reminding us, and strengthening our nerve, when we make even the smallest decisions.

Week Eight: SATURDAY

More of God Can Use Anybody: James

Take a Look: Matthew 20:17–28

"Whoever wants to become great among you must be your servant, and whoever wants to be first must be your slave."

Matthew 20:26–27

Thinking about James reminds me of an old college friend of mine, who became the pastor of a small-town church. When I asked him how he ended up there, he said, "I decided it would be a smart move for me at this point in my career."

Career. That word kind of bothered me. Of course, the ministry *is* a career, a profession. People get paid for it, and they have ambitions for themselves and their families. But usually you think of the ministry in terms of a *calling,* with pastors going to churches because they feel some kind of divine leading. A career is something you climb to the top of. A ministry is a matter of servanthood.

This is what makes a lot of people uncomfortable with some TV preachers. These guys may be sincere, but they seem so driven to get a bigger audience and draw attention to themselves that people wonder if they really want to help people or if all they're after is money, fame, and power.

It's a question you could fairly ask about James. Jesus called James and his brother John "sons of thunder." Some Bible scholars say Jesus used this term because they were ambitious guys with quick tempers. Pushy. When some people in a Samaritan village refused to receive Jesus, these two wanted to command fire to come down from heaven and consume the villagers (Luke 9:51–56). In today's reading, James and John come to Jesus with their mother to ask for special places in Christ's kingdom. Most people would call that pushy. Not only pushy but downright tacky.

Still, it was James and John, the sons of thunder, and Peter, the impulsive loudmouth, who were especially close to Jesus. Why? Maybe because sometimes that kind of "pushiness" is what's needed to get things done. Eventually James proved that his heart was in the right place. He became the first one of the original Twelve to be killed for his faith.

The truth is, ambition is a good thing. Pushy people can be hard to take, especially in a church or youth group setting. But God can put this kind of energy to good use in building his kingdom. Whether you go into full-time Christian work or not, you can have a "career" of faith and ministry. With a little drive, you can really get some good things done in your church and community. You can start by getting involved in your church youth group or local youth club. You might become an officer or head up a committee. But just remember to let *God* manage your career. Make it your goal to push *his* agenda, not your own.

WEEK NINE

Week Nine: SUNDAY

God: Loving

Take a Look: John 3:1–21

"For God so loved the world that he gave his one and only Son, that whoever believes in him shall not perish but have eternal life."

John 3:16

I grew up as a P.K. (Preacher's Kid). I don't know what it's like nowadays, but back then you were supposed to be an example; people were watching. Good behavior (or non-bad behavior) seemed to be the big thing in the Christian life. Everything else was frosting.

So after I became a Christian at age six and as I got older, salvation seemed to me—even though I could recite John 3:16 and knew that God had made a huge sacrifice in sending his Son to die for my sins—kind of like a college scholarship: if I didn't keep my "grades" up, I might lose it. I didn't think of God loving me but of him watching me as others did: judging, keeping score, waiting for me to slip.

I wasn't in the habit of confessing sins as they happened. I was too scared of God to do that. I'd wait until they piled up so high that I couldn't stand the guilt anymore. Then I'd pray, "Lord, I promise—from now on I'll be good. Straight as an arrow, yessir. Clean slate. Fresh start. Just don't punish me." But not long afterward I'd be back in the same spot. "Really, Lord, I *mean* it this time. Honest!" Guess how long it lasted?

I always imagined God looking down on me and shaking his head, saying, "Hmph. Sinned again, eh? Well, I guess I'll just have to give you a few more zits."

Of course, Christians are supposed to live in a way that pleases God. But I had it backward. I was trying to keep my nose clean to *earn* God's love and acceptance. I had forgotten the gospel—the good news that God looked down from those ivory palaces, saw me for who I was, and decided to love and forgive me anyway. It was a love I could *never* earn, and only when I understood that would I have the freedom and power to live like Christ.

It wasn't until my first year of college that I began to discover that God was not a slave driver but a loving Father. He wanted me to get off my guilt trip and start enjoying the new life he had made possible for me. He was *approachable*—someone I could go to with my frustrations and failures. Becoming convinced of God's unconditional love for me was my first step in getting to know him as my heavenly Father—the relationship we were always meant to have.

Like Nicodemus, in today's Scripture reading, I finally understood that through Jesus, God delivered a revolutionary idea—that human beings could be born again, given a fresh start, freed from the chains of sin and guilt.

God didn't send Jesus into the world to zap you but to save you. He loves you. And that's something to smile about!

Week Nine: MONDAY

Does Anybody Really Know What Time It Is?

Take a Look: Acts 1:1–11

> *"It is not for you to know the times or dates the Father has set by his own authority."*
>
> *Acts 1:7*

Today's reading tells the amazing story of the day Jesus ascended into heaven. One minute he was talking with his disciples, and the next he was rising up into a cloud and disappearing. The disciples stood there with their mouths hanging open, staring up into space. They had been with Jesus three years. After his resurrection, it looked as if anything were possible. And now he was gone. They must have felt as if the rug had been pulled out from under them. But the two men in white who appeared beside them promised that Jesus would return to set up his kingdom—*someday.*

Someday. But when? That question has been argued for centuries. It's amazing how cocky some people are when it comes to Bible prophecy. They read the prophetic books of Daniel and Revelation, look at events in the Middle East, and are sure they've figured out when Jesus Christ will come back. They enjoy feeling that they have the scoop on the future.

Unfortunately, this kind of cockiness can lead to embarrassment—and worse. I have on my shelf a book entitled *Eighty-eight Reasons Why the Rapture Will Be in 1988.* This title refers to the day when Christians will be "caught up to meet the Lord in the air." I'm guessing the book has dropped off the best-seller list by now.

But it's not just a matter of looking stupid. David Koresh, leader of the Branch Davidian cult in Waco, Texas, was obsessed with the "end times." His fear of persecution caused him to stockpile a huge arsenal of weapons, leading to a confrontation with government authorities and eventually to dozens of men, women, and children dying in a fire.

Don't get me wrong. Bible prophecy is an interesting subject. Christians should know what the Bible says about it and look forward to the Lord's return. But we shouldn't let it take our attention from what we're really supposed to be doing.

As Jesus told his disciples in Acts 1, "It is not for you to know the times or dates the Father has set by his own authority" (v. 7). Instead of setting up his kingdom on earth right then, he would send them the Holy Spirit, and his disciples would become his witnesses in the world, building the church. And now that's our job.

What a promise! Someday—and it could be anytime—Jesus will return and be acknowledged by everyone as the King of Kings and Lord of Lords. Until then we shouldn't waste time trying to figure out *when*. We should be making the most of being Christ's witnesses in our world each day.

Week Nine: TUESDAY

The People's Choice

Take a Look: Romans 13:1–14

There is no authority except that which God has established.

Romans 13:1

When Paul writes in Romans 13 about the Christian's attitude toward government, he says that no matter what government system Christians live under, they should live as Christians. That means doing good: obeying the laws, respecting authority, paying taxes, honoring public officials (vv. 3, 7)—basically, living up to your responsibilities as a citizen. That's important, because all authority is established by God (v. 1)—even in those who do a lousy job.

This message may have been hard for the Christians in Rome to swallow. They didn't have anywhere near the freedoms we enjoy today. In fact, the Roman government ended up being one of the biggest persecutors of the early church. We're fortunate to live in a different time, in a country that guarantees our freedoms of speech and religion.

We have a democratic system, in which everybody gets a chance to be heard—a privilege that includes the right to vote. Using these freedoms is part of being a good citizen.

I've always been nuts about politics, even before I was voting age. Maybe you are, too. There can be a lot of excitement in following candidates and seeing how elections come out, whether it's a local, state, or national election. It can be a fun hobby. But it can also be heartbreak. What do you do when your favorite candidate for president—or senator or governor or village clerk—bites the dust early? Do you pick up your marbles and go home? Maybe you lose interest in politics altogether—your candidate didn't make it, so what's the point?

Well, the point is that whether we're voting age or not, elections ask us to do something we don't always like to do. They make us *choose*—at least in our own minds—who should be elected. Sometimes it seems as if we're forced to choose "the lesser of two evils." That's bound to happen. Politics is an imperfect process that elects imperfect people to lead an imperfect nation. We'd like things to be a little more cut and dried, but we're still stuck with a choice.

That's why it's important for Christians to get informed and get involved. Whatever issues are most important to you—peace, justice, racial equality, religious freedom, abortion, drugs—one of the candidates in any election could take your country, state, or community in a direction *closer* to where you believe it should go. It can be a tough choice, but that's politics.

Maybe you'd rather ignore politics. That's a choice, too. But with the government taking a bite out of your part-time paycheck and with not much time before you're eligible for the military draft, it's never too early to find out what your government is up to and make your opinions known. Unlike the Christians at Rome, we have the chance to *shape* the government whose laws and rulers we obey. The choices we make today may determine the choices we have tomorrow.

Week Nine: **WEDNESDAY**

Clashing Symbols

Take a Look: 1 Corinthians 1:18–31

*God chose the foolish things of the world to shame the
wise.*

1 Corinthians 1:27

Over the years, state legislatures in the United States
have passed laws designating their state symbols. Almost
every state in the Union has a state flower, tree, bird, song,
and nickname. But a few states have really gone all out.

Maryland, for example, has a state sport—jousting.
That's where two guys on horseback duke it out—with
lances.

The state beverage of Massachusetts is cranberry juice.
Ohio's is tomato juice.

New Mexico's state vegetables are the chile and the
frijole.

Utah's state emblem is the beehive.

Connecticut boasts a state hero, Nathan Hale, and a
state horse, the Appaloosa.

Do you collect seashells? North Carolina's state shell
is the Scotch Bonnet. Virginia's is the oyster shell.

Western wheat grass is the state grass of South Dakota.

But my own state of Nebraska should win the prize for
imagination. The legislature has not only designated the
mammoth as the state fossil but even chosen a state *soil*. I'm
told it's a lot better than regular dirt.

Silly? Foolish? Lame? Maybe. But all of these symbols
point to things a state's citizens are really proud of. They're
meant to represent a unique history and character.

As Christians, we also have a symbol—the *cross*. You see it everywhere—inside churches, on top of churches, on necklaces, earrings, lapel pins, tombstones.

When you think about it, it seems a little weird. The cross was an instrument of *execution for criminals*. People back in the first century saw it, in the words of the old hymn, as "the emblem of suffering and shame." If Jesus had been executed in modern times, we might have little electric chairs on top of our churches and on our lapels. Then folks would think we were really wacky!

That's the attitude Paul ran into while preaching the gospel. In 1 Corinthians 1, he says the cross was a stumbling block to the Jews and foolishness to the Gentiles (v. 23). Some people just couldn't understand why anybody would worship a guy who had been crucified—a *loser*.

But Paul made no apologies for the cross. It symbolized something more than suffering and shame. It was a symbol of God's love and forgiveness. It showed Jesus' attitude of courage and sacrifice, and the drastic action needed to redeem humankind.

In two thousand years, many people have forgotten what the cross really means; they've come to see it as a pretty little charm you wear on a chain around your neck. But it wasn't pretty. Christ's death on the cross was a gruesome injustice. But to save us from our sins, it was necessary.

Pray now and thank God for the cross and for his Son, who faced it bravely. Then make a brand-new commitment to pick up your own "cross" and follow him (Matt. 16:24–25).

Week Nine: THURSDAY

What's Your Part?

Take a Look: 1 Corinthians 12

The body is not made up of one part but of many.
1 Corinthians 12:14

About twenty years ago a TV show called *The Six Million Dollar Man* featured an astronaut named Steve Austin. Steve had a terrible crash, and scientists fixed him up with six million dollars' worth of bionic spare parts.

Recently the science of body repair has taken some Steve Austin–like leaps, with something called free-flap surgery. This surgery doesn't involve artificial materials but skin, muscles, bone, and cartilage taken from a patient's own body.

Let's say you fall while rollerblading and royally mess up your nose. No problem. A plastic surgeon can build a new one for you out of your own tissues, attached to another part of your body—say, your forearm. That way, the tissue will be kept healthy and out of sight (assuming you wear long sleeves) during construction. Once the nose is finished, the doctor can move it to where it belongs, using microsurgery techniques. And since it's all *you*, there's no chance of your body rejecting the tissue.

Of course, this kind of surgery has its limits. It won't build you a new arm or leg—there's not enough of you to go around for that. But for smaller repair jobs, it's the winner—by a nose!

Bodies are important. Try living without one. When Paul calls the church the *body of Christ*, he's using the perfect illustration.

First, the church is a *diverse* thing, like the body—lots of different parts and functions. There are lots of jobs to fill in the local church, requiring all kinds of talents.

Second, every part of a body needs the other parts in order to function. Try lifting your arm above your head without your shoulder joint, for example. In the church, things get harder when one or more members stop doing their part.

Third, the church physically does the kind of things Jesus would do if he were still physically present on earth—preaching, feeding, healing, helping, serving. As members of a church, we are literally the eyes, ears, mouth, hands, and feet of Christ, for each other and for our world.

What part of the body are you? What spiritual gifts do you have that you can use in the church? It's an important question, because there's a fourth way the church is like a body: when one part gets separated from the rest, it grows cold and dies. Why does that plastic surgeon build a new nose for you with tissues attached to your forearm? Because the new part needs a blood supply, oxygen, life. When you stop going to church or stop being involved, you start to lose some of the spiritual life that comes from worship, work, and fellowship with other Christians.

The church is the body of Christ. What's your part? Ask God to show you.

Week Nine: FRIDAY

The Best Hope

Take a Look: 1 Corinthians 15:20–58

> *The last enemy to be destroyed is death.*
> 1 Corinthians 15:26

"Man is destined to die once, and after that to face judgment," said the writer of Hebrews (9:27). Ouch. No doubt about it, death makes us uncomfortable. We don't like to think about it much, and while we're very young, it's easy not to. We have all of life ahead of us—we think.

But sooner or later death touches our lives. A favorite pet, a friend, or maybe a family member dies, and all of a sudden we're dealing with feelings and emotions we've never had before. And the truths we learned in Sunday school and church about handling death are hard to believe, at least for a while. Grief is a powerful thing.

Remember my friend Kevin, the private pilot with whom I got caught in a Rocky Mountain cloud bank, back in week 1? We could have crashed, but with guidance from the control tower, Kevin landed our plane safely. He was a good pilot. But his skill would only take him so far. While I was writing this book, I learned that Kevin and a friend had been killed when his plane crashed in an ice storm, only a few miles from their destination. Half a dozen kids were left fatherless.

It seemed so unbelievable. Death wasn't supposed to happen to people my age. But once again I was faced with the fact that death is a part of life.

Everybody has to learn to deal with death—even the rich and famous. A TV actress who lost her sister told *People* magazine, "I guess I don't believe that death is the end. I think I've digested it in my own way. I believe that my sister is somewhere, and that is a calming idea."

She apparently thinks there is some kind of afterlife— some kind of future—after death seemingly brings things to a grinding halt. The idea makes her feel better. And although she probably wasn't thinking about it when she said it, her comment goes right along with Paul's writing about the Christian's future beyond the grave.

Except that in 1 Corinthians 15 Paul is much, much more definite. Like Jesus, we're destined for *resurrection* and eternity with God in heaven, and a reunion with people we love. For a Christian, Paul says, death not only isn't the end—it's a victorious new *beginning*. Someday our bodies will be brought back to life in a perfect, spiritual form. It's like planting a seed: a dry, apparently lifeless chunk of matter springs up and becomes a beautiful plant.

Loving someone and then losing them to death is the hardest thing you will ever do. As you grieve, you may go through stages of denial, anger, and depression. But acceptance may come a little more easily if you hang on to the hope you have as a Christian: death isn't the end, it's a beginning. And when a fellow believer dies, it's not "Goodbye," it's "See you soon."

Week Nine: SATURDAY

God Can Use Anybody, Chapter Nine: James, Son of Alphaeus

Take a Look: Ephesians 4:7–16

Speaking the truth in love, we will in all things grow up into him.
                                              Ephesians 4:15

Short people got no reason to live.
          from "Short People" by Randy Newman

"It's finally happened," I can hear you saying. "Johnson's gone nuts. He's picked a Scripture reading that doesn't even mention today's apostle, and then he drags in a line from some easy-listening song from the 1970s. The pressure must be getting to him."

Well, I haven't gone nuts. At least not yet. Give me a chance to hook it all together.

James, the son of Alphaeus, is referred to in the New Testament as James the *Less,* or James the *Little* (Mark 15:40 NASB). The Greek word used here for *little* can mean "younger" (NIV), but it can also mean "short." Bible scholars believe that James, the son of Alphaeus, might have been a short guy.

We'll never know for sure, because we don't know much about James the Less. He's another one of those unsung heroes of the faith who faded into obscurity after Jesus left the scene. But if it's true that he was, shall we say, *diminutive of stature* (look it up yourself—you'll remember it longer), then he had one big strike against him: folks tend to favor tall people over the, uh, *vertically challenged.*

It's true. Research has shown that tall people seem to do better in life. They make a bigger impression. They get more attention, get jobs more easily, get dates more easily, and on and on and on. Often, being short means being passed by and passed over. People don't take you as seriously. And you get stuck with nicknames like Shorty, Pee-Wee, and James the Less.

Randy Newman's song "Short People" was written to expose this kind of prejudice.

It's not fair, of course. Physical characteristics, especially height, can be hard to do anything about. And outward appearances aren't what really count, anyway. It's what's *inside* you that's most important.

And that's where today's reading comes in. In Ephesians 4, Paul writes that it's not so important to grow tall physically as it is to grow up spiritually. God gives us spiritual gifts so that we can use them to build up the church and grow up to maturity—"attaining to the whole measure of the fullness of Christ" (v. 13). In other words, when it comes to true stature, God uses a different yardstick; he measures on the inside, not the outside. He wants us to

grow up to be like his Son—mature, wise, sensitive, coura-
geous, able to handle life.

No matter what your height, you can grow tall in
Christ.

WEEK
TEN

Week Ten: SUNDAY

God: Truthful

Take a Look: Psalm 111

> *The works of his hands are faithful and just.*
> *Psalm 111:7*

When Hurricane Andrew hit in 1992, south Florida took a beating. The cost of the damage in lives and property was enormous, with thousands of people killed, injured, or left homeless.

What surprised many people was that so many houses were blown away—*new* houses, which supposedly were built to specifications that would stand up to high winds. What had gone wrong with those buildings?

The problem was the builders. While some of them had built their houses to the new specs and followed the law exactly, others had not. They rushed the job, using inferior materials and construction techniques. Still, they sold the houses as the "new and improved" kind. To put it bluntly? They *lied.*

The result of their lie was that the damage was much worse than it might have been. The houses looked good, but they fell apart when put to the test.

Truth and honesty are important to us every day. They can mean the difference between safety and disaster, because truthfulness goes together with quality. Think about it. We want the food we buy at the supermarket to be pure and nutritious. To make sure of that, the government requires "truth in labeling." A product's label has to describe exactly what's in it. And that's important—we eat enough junk food without the good stuff being junk without our knowing it.

Quality—that's what the writer of Psalm 111 is talking about when he praises God's works. "The works of his hands are faithful and just," says verse 7. That means that God builds truth and quality into everything he says and does. His works and his Word can be depended upon. They're rock solid. So when the Bible makes promises like, "The LORD is near to all who call on him, to all who call on him in truth" (Ps. 145:18), you can count on him to be there for you.

How are you doing in the truth-and-honesty department? Usually we think of truth in terms of what we say, but there's just as much of a truth test in what we do or appear to do. One of the worst things we can do as Christians is to say one thing and do another.

Keep tapping into God's truth. Never give up on reading the Bible, praying, worshiping, or talking about spiritual things with your friends. The more you get acquainted with God's truth, the more you'll start showing it yourself.

Week Ten: MONDAY

The Invaders

Take a Look: 1 Peter 5:6–11

> *Your enemy the devil prowls around like a roaring lion looking for someone to devour.*
>
> *1 Peter 5:8*

Get ready to be, as they say, *grossed out.* Remember hearing about the killer bees? Nasty little insects working their way northward from South America. Well, now they have some playmates.

The Asian cockroach has shown up in the southern United States. Affectionately and scientifically known as *Blattela Asahanai,* the little pests are different from the German cockroach typically found in this country. Unlike their German relatives, they not only crawl, they can *fly.* And Asian cockroaches don't run for cover when you turn on the lights. In fact, they're *drawn* to light, so if you've got 'em, they'll follow you from room to room.

Don't think you'll get rid of them by turning off the lights, either. In darkness, they seek moisture—damp towels in the bathroom, for instance. Roach experts (try writing that next to "occupation" on a job application) aren't sure if they can stop the Asian roach from spreading. But until they can, sweet dreams.

"Yuk!" you say. "I thought this was a devotional book!"

Well, there is a reason for bringing up this rather nasty subject, and I promise I won't bring it up again.

Today's Scripture reading shows us a frightening image of Satan—a hungry lion looking for lunch. Peter is saying, "Don't take the Devil lightly; he's a beast, and he's out to get you."

Of course, resisting Satan would be a piece of cake if he were *always* a roaring lion. I mean, roaring lions are pretty easy to spot—and to avoid. But sometimes Satan is more like the Asian cockroach. He's sneaky. He likes to get inside things, such as your mind, your appetites. He knows your weak spots, the cracks where he can penetrate—maybe in what you read or watch or listen to.

He certainly isn't shy—he'll follow you wherever you go, if you let him. And once he's inside, his influence can multiply. It may breed silently in hiding for quite a while but then emerge in the worst places—your conversation, your relationships, your desires and dreams. And the desire for your own gratification is Satan's big weapon. He doesn't have to devour you from the outside if he thinks he can rot you from the inside.

Fortunately, you don't have to be alone in your fight against King Roach. First Corinthians 10:13 promises that God "will not let you be tempted beyond what you can bear. But when you are tempted, he will also provide a way out so that you can stand up under it."

Now, if you think I'm going to say that God is the ultimate can of Raid, you're crazy. But just remember that when it comes to resisting Satan, God doesn't expect us to be able to do what he doesn't *enable* us to do. Whether it's an attack of lions or roaches, God can show you the way out. Depend on it.

Week Ten: TUESDAY

Forces of Darkness

Take a Look: Ephesians 6:10–20

> *Our struggle is not against flesh and blood.*
> *Ephesians 6:12*

On Halloween night a few years ago, ABC's *World News Tonight* ran a story about a British businessman who runs a mail-order house for witches. With over one hundred thousand witches in England, there's a big market for his catalogs, from which they can order ingredients for magic potions and other trinkets and doodads, plus the official mumbo jumbo for casting spells.

The witches interviewed for the report pointed out that they're bending over backward to overcome the "negative-image problem" that led to many of their kind being barbecued by indignant citizens through the ages. Witchcraft, they claim, is now being used in more positive ways, to increase people's creativity and improve their love relationships.

As the report came to a close with scenes from a pagan ritual, the reporter made a bad pun about the *nouveau witch* (kind of like *nouveau riche*—get it?). Back in the studio, anchorman Peter Jennings gave his audience an amused smile and said, "Good night."

And that's how a lot of people view witches and other practitioners of the "occult sciences." They're seen as merely eccentric—about as menacing as a bunch of fraternity guys swallowing goldfish. A joke.

As Christians, we can't dismiss the occult so easily. Ephesians 6:11–12 warns us that we really are on the front lines of a life-and-death spiritual battle with the bad guys—the forces of darkness. And spiritual warfare is serious business.

It's especially serious because the occult has become *big* business—a billion-dollar industry luring people into a kingdom controlled by Satan. Books, magazines, and cassette tapes are available on every occult subject—witchcraft, astrology, fortune-telling, demonology, communicating with the dead, magic, ghosts, Satan worship. This material gives the occult a kind of legitimacy. Because we see so much of it everywhere, people begin to think of the occult as a hobby, like gardening or collecting comic books.

But it's not so harmless. Police authorities are nervous about the spread of Satanism. Satanists believe in self-gratification and the destruction of anything good. They are preoccupied with death, and their secret rituals involve coffins, dead bodies, sexual abuse, and even cannibalism. Scary? You better believe it! And many people who start dabbling in the occult because they're simply curious about the secrets of life and death find it impossible to stop or get out.

The big message for Christians who wonder about the occult and fear its power is this: "The one who is in you is greater than the one who is in the world" (1 John 4:4). There is a real battle going on, but we don't have to fear the outcome if we'll "put on the full armor of God" and enlist with Jesus Christ on the side of victory.

Week Ten: WEDNESDAY

Angels?

Take a Look: 1 Timothy 4

> *There will be false teachers among you.*
> *2 Peter 2:1*

I was sitting at home on a Saturday night when my roommate called to tell me he was bringing home some friends he had met. But I wasn't prepared for what I saw when he and his "friends" arrived: two dirty young men, unshaved, barefoot, and wearing robes made from white percale bedsheets. I found out they were the followers of a carpenter from California who claimed to be Jesus Christ returned to the earth. Weird.

They called themselves "the Brothers," but people in the towns they traveled through knew them affectionately as "the Angels." My roommate, Keith, fun-lover and philosophy student, had thought it might be neat to invite them over for a bit of chitchat. As we all sat down in the living room, I shot my roommate a look that said what Moe used to say to Larry and Curly when they had done something especially aggravating: *Remind me to kill you later.*

We quickly found out what the Angels believed. You couldn't get married or have sex; celibacy was the thing. You couldn't eat meat, fish, eggs, or milk products; animals were our fellow souls on the way to heaven. Their "messiah," the paint-and-drywall guy from California, rolled his own cigarettes from Bugler brand tobacco, and they did, too. In fact, many spiritual and prophetic insights were to be gleaned from the label of the Bugler tobacco can. Double weird.

They were convinced that their beliefs were consistent with the Bible, but when we tried to point out contradictions, they said, "How do *you* know? That book was written two thousand years ago."

Obviously, we weren't in for a blessed time of fellowship with the Brothers, so they left—but not until they'd conned us out of a shower, a night's sleep under our roof, and a box of cereal.

It wasn't until later that the words of 1 Timothy 4:3 hit me like a freight train: "They forbid people to marry and order them to abstain from certain foods, which God created to be received with thanksgiving by those who believe and who know the truth." I had seen a biblical prophecy fulfilled in my own living room. I had met up with the kind of false religion that was predicted for the "latter times."

God is in the truth business. It's not the only thing he does, but it's one of his main lines. God showed us himself and his plan to save humankind in Jesus Christ. He gets real testy when somebody screws up the facts. So all through the New Testament, we get warnings about false prophets and teachers who twist the story to suit their own purposes. The only way to get it straight is to go straight to the Bible and check it out for yourself; then you'll know what to believe.

Week Ten: THURSDAY

The Faith Debate

Take a Look: 1 Peter 3:13–22

> *Be prepared to give an answer to everyone who asks*
> *you to give the reason for the hope that you have.*
> *1 Peter 3:15*

On a bus trip to Arkansas in the summer of my junior year, I overheard a conversation across the aisle from me. The man talking turned out to be a member of the Baha'i faith, a cult. He was complaining to the woman next to him about being mistreated by "fanatical" Christians.

"I know what you mean," the woman said. "I'm a Jehovah's Witness."

"Really?" the man responded, interested. "Baha'is believe that all the world's religions are one. We take the best from all of them."

The man sitting in front of them (a Baptist preacher I had met earlier) turned around, glared at them, and sternly quoted Solomon in his best King James tone: "There is a way which seemeth right unto a man, but the end thereof are the ways of death" (Prov. 14:12).

"What's that?" asked the Baha'i.

"That's the Bible, God's Word," the preacher stated. "If you don't believe in the Bible, you're lost."

"But how can you believe all those stories in the Bible? What about that Methuselah guy? Didn't he live ten thousand years or something?"

"Nine hundred sixty-nine years," I blurted out. I winced. My Sunday school–trained spiritual autopilot had just kicked in. Soon I was roped into the discussion across the aisle, and I felt obligated to defend the faith by *winning this argument.*

"How can you just pick and choose what you want to believe?" I challenged. "What about *truth*? What do you do with the Ten Commandments, for example?"

The Baha'i brightened. "Oh, we accept the teachings of Moses, too. We're very open-minded."

The woman sitting behind me cut in. From her questions, it was clear to me she was Jewish. "If you accept the teachings of Moses," she began, "how can you ignore the history of the Old Testament?"

As the Baha'i talked around this one, I fetched the Bible from my carry-on bag and began flipping pages, looking for the Big Answer. But then I realized I had no idea what I was looking for. I had thought that, armed with just my wits and the Word of God, I could shame any scoffer. Now I wasn't so sure.

The discussion eventually died, with nothing settled. I leaned back and thought about what had just happened. In two rows on a Greyhound bus sat a Baptist preacher, a Baha'i, a Jehovah's Witness, and a Jew, all holding competing beliefs. It was a lot like the world—complex and bound to invite conflict. Witnessing for Christ in a world like that had to be more than beating people down and winning arguments.

In today's reading, Peter says we may suffer for our faith, but we're supposed to "be prepared to give an answer to everyone who asks ... with gentleness and respect" (v. 15). That means knowing and saying what we believe, without apologies but in a gentle way that respects the feelings of others.

Week Ten: FRIDAY

Rich and Famous

Take a Look: 1 Timothy 6:6–19

> *The love of money is a root of all kinds of evil.*
> *1 Timothy 6:10*

If you live in America and have a TV set, sooner or later you're going to see an episode of *Lifestyles of the Rich and Famous*. The show's been on for over ten years, and host Robin Leach never tires of showing viewers how the "better half" lives. Usually we see some TV or movie star at home in their mansion or out on their yacht or flying somewhere in their private jet. It all looks very nice and luxurious and trouble-free.

But *Lifestyles* hasn't escaped its share of bad press. Critics charge that the program glorifies greed. To which Robin Leach cheerfully pleads guilty. "The show is about the worship of money," Robin told *TV Guide*. "*I* worship money. I'm a great believer in capitalism. I think Americans have got to understand why capitalism works and socialism doesn't."

Capitalism? Socialism? It's pretty confusing. But Robin Leach himself has made a pile of money making us envy the rich and famous. That's the only reason his show stays on the air—because people like to fantasize about being wealthy. Human beings are born fantasizers. We imagine that money will solve all our problems.

It reminds me of something former talk show host Johnny Carson once said about money (and he's loaded): "The only problem money solves is the problem of not having enough money. It doesn't make you stronger. It doesn't make you smarter. It doesn't make your relationships any better." Someone else once said that a miserable poor person is really better off than a miserable rich person: the poor person at least has hope that money will help.

But what Paul is driving home to Timothy, in today's Scripture reading, is that money isn't the answer—contentment is. Longing for more money can cause us to wander from the faith (v. 10). It takes our energy and attention away from our real goals of righteousness, faith, and love and makes us self-absorbed and competitive. Learning thankfulness and contentment with what we have will help us focus on the more important things.

OK, OK, money isn't evil *in itself*. It comes in plenty handy, and there are lots of good Christians with fat wallets. But Paul warns them, in verses 17–19, that they should also be rich in good works, being generous and willing to share. See? Our obligations never stop, even if we get rich.

Remember: The only problem money solves is the problem of not having enough money. God has even more important things for you to work for.

Week Ten: SATURDAY

God Can Use Anybody: Simon the Zealot

Take a Look: Titus 2:11–3:7

> . . . *a people that are his very own, eager to do what is good.*
>
> *Titus 2:14*

One of my friends attended junior high in Minneapolis when racial tensions started to heat up. A few black students in the school had harassed and beaten up some white kids. When they were hauled before a special meeting of the student council to account for their actions, the offenders said they were protesting against what they said were racist history books used in the school.

"Sorry," said one of the students who had been assaulted. "But we didn't write those history books."

A fair point. Those black students were mad, and they had every right to disagree with how the school taught the history of African-Americans. They wanted to change things. But they were pointing their anger and energy in the wrong direction; hurting their classmates wasn't going to make the history books any more fair.

This isn't a *racial* thing, it's a *human* thing. When we're really mad, physical violence feels good, in a sick kind of way. But it rarely does any good. That's why it's better to go for a run or go to a driving range and hit a bucket of golf balls than take out our anger on other people. Violence only makes things worse.

Simon the Zealot was a man with a history of violence. He's not mentioned much in the Scriptures, but most Bible scholars agree that the tag *Zealot* (Matt. 10:4) means he was a member of a fanatical group who wanted to overthrow the Roman government by force. These guys would terrorize the countryside, causing trouble and bloodshed wherever they went—anything to hassle the hated Romans, who controlled the land and lives of the Jews.

Of course, *Zealot* is based on the word *zeal*—an almost jealous desire or passion for something. Simon had a zeal for the freedom of Israel. He wanted a revolution.

But it wasn't until he met Jesus that he became a real revolutionary. Jesus wasn't offering a violent or military solution to people's problems. He wanted to free them spiritually—one person at a time. Apparently, Simon bought into this. He may already have learned, the hard way, that violence doesn't work.

Why would Jesus choose Simon? Because he wanted people with zeal, that burning passion that makes them work hard for something over the long haul. Only now Simon's passion was channeled in a new, positive direction.

In today's reading, Paul tells Titus to remind people in the church that Jesus had chosen them as well. Now they should be "eager [some translations say *zealous*] to do what is good" (2:14) and be "peaceable and considerate" (3:2). Only with the Holy Spirit's help can you be zealous and peaceable at the same time.

Ask the Spirit to give you zeal, fire, passion, for what Jesus wants you to do.

WEEK ELEVEN

Week Eleven: SUNDAY

God: Wise

Take a Look: Proverbs 8

> *"I [wisdom] was there when he set the heavens in place."*
>
> *Proverbs 8:27*

You know, planet Earth has a lot of problems—war, disease, pollution, famine—but as planets go, it's still a pretty good neighborhood.

Consider our closest neighbors in the solar system, Mars and Venus. Venus is closer to the Sun and too hot to sustain life. Mars is farther away from the Sun and extremely cold. Its atmosphere is too thin to block lethal doses of the Sun's ultraviolet radiation. Bottom line—no life on Mars either.

But Earth is . . . well, just right. It's just the right distance from the Sun so that it's not too hot and not too cold (yeah, even in Nebraska winters). Its atmosphere is thick enough to shut out killing radiation and preserve water, oxygen, and plants. Earth is the only planet in our solar system—and for all we know, in the whole universe—where human and animal life is even possible, let alone likely.

When you think about it, people who argue for evolution and a Creator-less universe have a pretty tough job. "See, there just happened to be this Big Bang, and all these big chunks of matter just happened to become stars and planets, and one of them happened to end up just the right distance from the Sun, and over billions of years just happened to develop an atmosphere. And in another few billion years, a little fish-kinda-thing just *happened* to crawl up out of the slime and turn into a mammal and then into an ape and then into a human. See?"

Christians take a slightly different view. God cut out the middleman and just *created* the whole works.

What does wisdom have to do with creation? In Proverbs 8 wisdom tells us herself. In verses 22–31 she brags, "Before God even got the universe rolling, I was there." God's wisdom was necessary for creation. Why? Because wisdom gets the job done right, that's why.

Wisdom puts Earth exactly the right distance from the Sun. Wisdom puts the right gases in the atmosphere, and the right number of genes in your body. Wisdom goes beyond just knowing everything; it's a matter of using that knowledge in the right way. The perfect way. The best way.

God is the source of all wisdom. And he's been nice enough to cut off a big slice of it and serve it up in the form of the Bible. That's why studying the Bible is so important. It helps us to learn how to get the job—the job of living life—done right.

Proverbs is a book of wisdom. And so is the very practical book of James. Over the next couple of weeks, we'll find out what James has to say about living life. In the meantime, remember: this planet never would have made it if God hadn't had the wisdom to do the job right.

Week Eleven: MONDAY

Mysterious Ways

Take a Look: James 1:1–18

> *Every good and perfect gift is from above.*
> *James 1:17*

Up to now, I'd have to say that 1982 was the worst year of my life. And the best. And in terms of overall weirdness, it ranks in the top two.

I was unemployed at a time when there were no jobs to be found. I was getting sixty dollars a week unemployment compensation and was living in a roach-infested, $120-per-month, furnished apartment. I did a little of everything. I took temporary jobs. I donated blood plasma twice a week. I volunteered as a human guinea pig at a pharmaceutical lab. I was living below the poverty level for the first time in my life.

Now it gets *really* weird.

I was in between unemployment checks, and I had only four dollars to my name. I went to the store and bought four dollars' worth of groceries. After I put away my macaroni and cheese (a daily staple), green beans, cheap bread, and generic peanut butter, I sat down and bawled my eyes out. I had no job, no prospects, and my unemployment would soon run out. I'd reached the end of the line.

I flopped down on my bed and prayed. "God, I've run out of ideas. I don't know what to do. All I know is that I can't worry about it anymore. You'll have to do something somehow."

And that was it. I can't say I made a deeper spiritual commitment at that point, and I didn't ask for anything specific, but in desperation I was "casting my burden on the Lord."

I felt surprisingly better. I stopped worrying. As far as I was concerned, anything that happened was OK with me.

Strange things began to occur. Like the time I found twenty dollars under the windshield wiper of my car. Hmmm. Or the time I needed another sixty dollars to pay my rent and found exactly that amount in cash in my mailbox. Hmmm again.

But the strangest incident was the day I went to the bank with my very last unemployment check. In the bank lobby

I ran into a childhood pal of mine. When I told him I was unemployed, he told me about a job in his computer firm.

I started work at the company two weeks later. I never went hungry, and I never went without anything I really needed.

How did it all happen? I don't know. I think we make a mistake when we try to figure out how God makes his moves. All we really need to know is what James says on the subject: "Every good and perfect gift is from above, coming down from the Father of the heavenly lights, who does not change like shifting shadows" (1:17).

If something is good, then you gotta *know* God had something to do with it!

Week Eleven: TUESDAY

Just Do It

Take a Look: James 1:19–27

Do not merely listen to the word, and so deceive your-selves. Do what it says.

James 1:22

I was chosen to play the lead in my eighth-grade drama class play. What could I say? I was a natural actor. (Yeah, this was the disastrous Christmas play I told you about back in week 7. You can imagine how *this* story turns out.)

One morning, my drama teacher and I rehearsed my "blocking"—where I would stand, sit, and move onstage. She knew exactly what she wanted: pause here, sit down there, cross over here. We walked through it a few times, and I said, "Got it. No problem." I hadn't taken any notes. I figured I'd remember it. I was a natural.

Well, as you may remember, I blew it—forgot the whole thing. Actually, the blocking turned out to be the least of my worries. I guess I wasn't such a "natural," after all.

James gives some pretty interesting instructions for living: "Be quick to listen, slow to speak and slow to become angry" (v. 19)—precisely because those things *don't* come naturally. If we say, "Got it. No problem," but don't work at obeying those instructions—"doing" the Word—our performance will suffer. We're not the natural Christians we think we are.

One of the worst traps a Christian can fall into is to think that just believing the right things is enough. It isn't. The Bible is the best tool we have, but it means practically nothing to our real lives if we don't use it.

The Word of God is the best "acting" course there is. How's your performance coming?

Week Eleven: WEDNESDAY

Playing Favorites

Take a Look: James 2:1–13

> *As believers in our glorious Lord Jesus Christ, don't show favoritism.*
>
> *James 2:1*

A large church I know of started a bus ministry to pick up new kids for Sunday school. In numbers, at least, it was a big success. Every week, the people watched Sunday school attendance climb. "What a neat outreach!" they said. Everybody felt good about it.

Then on rally day, the small-fry Sunday school classes sang a special song from the choir loft, and people actually saw a bunch of those bus kids for the first time. There were a lot of black faces in that choir loft. Some of the kids were dirty, poor, and not dressed very well. A few important people in the congregation started to wonder out loud if this bus thing was such a good idea, after all. Apparently, only white, middle-class, well-dressed kids were welcome in their church.

James says that kind of attitude puts a smear on the name *Christian*. After all, when Jesus reached out to help people, he didn't look for designer labels or major credit cards. He opened his arms to all who believed.

Your church or youth group is a place where Christ wants you to extend his reach—to *everybody*. Not just the beautiful people, not just the rich kids, not just the fun people who help us have a good time. But everybody.

Of course, it's only human nature to want to hang out with the beautiful people and overlook the ones who make us feel uncomfortable. But then, our sinful human nature is what Jesus came to save us from.

Be honest: Have you been playing favorites? If so, what do you plan to do about it?

Week Eleven: THURSDAY

Paid Up

Take a Look: James 2:14–26

> *As the body without the spirit is dead, so faith without deeds is dead.*
>
> *James 2:26*

If you plan to go away to college, you might end up eating your meals at the campus food service.

Now, there are two things you should know in advance about college cafeteria food. One, the quality of the food isn't always that great. And two, you'll eat *tons* of it. In their freshman year, most college students gain an average of fifteen pounds. I used to get a good laugh from freshman women who couldn't figure out why their clothes didn't fit anymore. One of them actually speculated that the clothes dryers in the dorm were hotter than the one in her basement back home, and that's why her jeans were shrinking.

Anyway, let me get to the real point here. At my college, I paid for my meals in advance, at the same time I paid for my tuition and room fees. The registrar would punch a hole through "first semester" on my student I.D. card, to prove my meals were paid for. Then I'd just flash my I.D. at the cafeteria cashier, and she'd let me through the serving line. She could see I was paid up.

In today's reading, James isn't saying that as Christians, we're saved by our good works. He's just saying that good works are the visible proof to others that our faith is for real.

Some Christians have unpunched I.D. cards. They say they're "paid up," but without visible proof, their I.D. is worthless, phony. They can't fool the Head Cashier.

Abraham and Rahab proved their faith by putting their happiness and security on the line. What can you do this week to prove that your faith is real?

Week Eleven: FRIDAY

Contaminated!

Take a Look: James 3:1–12

Can both fresh water and salt water flow from the same spring?

James 3:11

A town in my area has a big problem: its water wells have been contaminated by carbon tetrachloride. Nasty stuff. Causes cancer. And the town can't afford to dig new wells. So the people have to drink bottled water.

Get a glass of that well water from the kitchen tap, and it looks pure. But it's deadly. You can't avoid the poison by drinking just a little or by drinking from a pretty glass.

When James, in chapter 3, nails sins of the tongue—boasting, gossip, cursing, offending others—he's talking about a poison that pollutes all the way through. "How can you bless the Lord and curse others, from the same mouth?" he asks. The answer is, you can't—and still be sincere.

One of the most crushing embarrassments in my life happened when I was working on a library book-moving crew after leaving college. We had on our crew a couple of nineteen-year-olds who had recently been married and were always hanging on each other. One day when they weren't around, the rest of us started talking about them—how sickening their public displays of affection were and so on. What we didn't know was that they were standing behind some stacks nearby. When they came out and confronted us about what we had said, we were mortified, and nothing was ever the same after that. I hated myself for taking part in the gossip.

The words we use on the outside bubble up from attitudes deep inside. Staying close to God and his Word will
help us keep our attitudes fresh and clean.

Your mouth can be a fountain or a sewer. Your choice.

Week Eleven: SATURDAY

God Can Use Anybody: Thomas

Take a Look: John 20

*"Blessed are those who have not seen and yet have
believed."*

John 20:29

"I'll believe it when I see it." I've heard that line a million times. I've said it plenty of times myself, usually when
I had my doubts about somebody's ability to deliver on a
promise.

OK, I admit it—I'm a born skeptic. So it's pretty appro-
priate that I was named after the apostle Thomas. He was a
skeptic, too—critical, slow to believe, always seeing the
dark side of things.

We see a lot of this from Thomas, in the gospel of John.
In John 11, when Jesus wanted to travel back to Judea,
where the Jews had tried to stone him to death, Thomas
feared the worst. He said to the others, "Let us also go, that
we may die with him" (v. 16). In other words, "If the Master is determined to go back to Judea and get himself killed
by a mob, we might as well go along and die, too."

In John 14, at the Last Supper, Jesus told the Twelve that
he would be leaving soon to prepare a place for them. "You
know the way to the place where I am going," he said.
Thomas replied, "Lord, we don't know where you are going,

so how can we know the way?" (vv. 4–5). In other words, "What are you talking about? Until this minute, we didn't know you were going *anywhere*. Start talking sense!"

In today's reading, from John 20, without visible proof Thomas refused to believe that Jesus was alive. He didn't want anybody making a fool of him. But when he finally did see Jesus, he was convinced. "My Lord and my God!"

But Jesus' next words shamed Thomas to his toes: "Blessed are those who have not seen and yet have believed." Jesus was saying that sight isn't the only way to perceive truth.

This reminds me of the story of Helen Keller. Blind and deaf from the age of two, she got all of her information about the world from the senses of touch, taste, and smell. Not only did she receive an education but she became a writer and even learned how to speak.

Thomas, thinking that only seeing was believing, was just as handicapped. So why did Jesus pick him in the first place? Maybe because even though he was hard to convince, Thomas really was committed to finding the truth.

God created each of us with a spiritual sense that can be developed through our relationship with him. If we let our faith become too brain centered, we can miss out on some big spiritual benefits.

Are you frustrated by things about Christianity that aren't easily explained? Do you want final proof? Keep reading the Bible and praying and try to open up and trust the Holy Spirit to give you understanding and reassurance. That's when faith really becomes *faith*.

WEEK TWELVE

Week Twelve: SUNDAY

God: Here, There, and Everywhere

Take a Look: Psalm 145

> *The LORD is near to all who call on him.*
> *Psalm 145:18*

When one of my college professors was driving his family home from church one Sunday, he asked his four-year-old son what he had learned in Sunday school that morning. The boy replied, "We learned that God is a big, flat guy!"

Flat? A big, flat guy? The professor scanned through the Scriptures in his head, wondering what possible passage would have led to *that* conclusion. But with a few more questions, he got his answer. The Sunday school teacher had taught her class that God is everywhere—or *omnipresent,* as the theologians like to say. So in his four-year-old brain, the professor's son had pictured God as a "cosmic pancake"—a being spread so thin across the universe that he could be everywhere at once.

Not bad, for a four-year-old theologian. But there's really no way for humans to comprehend the hugeness of God. We can buy the idea that God is holy, loving, gracious, and truthful. We can even accept the fact that he's all-powerful and all-knowing. But when it comes to his ability to be two places at once, it gets a little harder to swallow.

It can help to look at it this way: Maybe God's knowledge and presence are *connected.* He can be said to be everywhere, because he knows *what's going on* everywhere. Or vice versa. Probably both. As I said, humans will never be able to grasp the whole thing.

In Psalm 145 David echoes what he said back in Psalm 139. "Where can I go from your Spirit? Where can I flee from your presence?" (139:7). "The LORD is near to all who call on him. . . . He hears their cry and saves them" (145:18–19). Because God is not bound by time and space, he's always present and available. He's with me right this second. And he's also there with you.

Think about it. Wherever you're reading this devotional, God is right there. Can you feel his presence? The more spiritually active and sensitive you get, the more you'll be able to feel him. One way to develop your sense of God's presence is going to church and having fellowship with other Christians. Jesus said, "Where two or three come together in my name, there am I with them" (Matt. 18:20). Your church or youth group is one of the best places to find and feel the presence of God.

Week Twelve: MONDAY

Better Than Smart

Take a Look: James 3:13–18

> *Who is wise and understanding among you? Let him show it by his good life, by deeds done in the humility that comes from wisdom.*
>
> *James 3:13*

It was a sultry summer evening, and I was sitting in the bleachers, watching my church softball team play a game under the lights. It was about the fourth inning, and we were up to bat.

The opposing pitcher lobbed a powder-puff pitch right over the plate, and our batter smashed a hard line drive toward the second baseman—who, unfortunately, didn't have his eyes on the action at that particular moment. The ball smacked him square in the forehead, and he staggered back into the darkness of the outfield, finally collapsing in the grass. Just like David and Goliath.

The batter was already running when he saw where his drive had landed, and as he rounded first base, he stopped in his tracks, looking over at the fallen player to make sure he was OK.

This angered a man sitting near me in the stands. He stood up, shouting, "Go! Go! Go on to third! Don't wait to see if he's all right! Take your base!" The runner went on to third base, looking over his shoulder at the sprawled second baseman the whole way. As the loudmouth sat back down, he was still griping, "You don't stop to see if the guy's all right. You get safe on base first. . . ."

This really, really bugged me. I mean, I suppose it's *smart* to take advantage of a player injury to get a few extra bases. It's one of the things that can help you win softball games. But what's *smart* isn't always what's *wise*. The batter's instincts were really good on this one. When he saw the second baseman fall, he knew in his gut that getting to third base wasn't the most important thing; the condition of the guy's head was.

In today's reading, James says that real wisdom doesn't mix with selfish ambition. In fact, he says that wisdom from above—from God—is marked by peace, gentleness, and mercy. These qualities always look for the best results for other people. They're the opposite of selfishness.

I don't remember if my church softball team won that game, and I don't really care. But I do know that some of the most unsportsmanlike conduct and bad attitudes I've ever seen have been displayed at church sports events. And that's kind of sick, isn't it—people getting all worked up and seeing another church as the enemy?

Whatever you do today, wherever you go, ask God for the wisdom to be a *positive* force. In the long run, it's better to be wise than just smart.

Week Twelve: TUESDAY

Fair Warning

Take a Look: James 4:1–10

Submit yourselves, then, to God. Resist the devil, and he will flee from you.

James 4:7

In the State of Washington in 1980, Mount Saint Helens blew its top. The long-dormant volcano erupted, burying everything within reach.

For weeks before the blast, scientists could tell from their testing equipment that there was going to be a major eruption that would threaten life anywhere close to the mountain. So everybody in the area was told to evacuate to a place of safety.

Practically everybody heeded the warning and left.

Everybody, that is, except an old guy named Harry Truman. He had lived in those mountains for years, and there had never been a volcanic eruption. He refused to believe the warnings. When the volcano blew, he and his home were buried without a trace.

Pretty grim, huh? But when we ignore warnings, we pay a price. James is giving an unmistakable warning in chapter 4. Up to this point in the book, he's been pretty mild-mannered about his advice. But now he really takes the gloves off. His main target is *lust*—that is, the desire to get things and pleasure at all costs.

Whoever James's first readers were, some of them apparently had a big problem with materialism, greed, and pleasure seeking. And their lusts had led to envy and quarreling. It all adds up to something called *worldliness*—taking on the values of the world around you, instead of the values of Christ. It's sure easy to fall into this. Seeking our own pleasure is the most natural, human thing in the world. Eating, drinking, sleeping, sex, or any other appetite—even *shopping*—can take too big a priority in our lives. And James is warning that getting out of balance like that leads to negative consequences. The worst part is that since the Holy Spirit lives inside us, we're making him compete for "space" with all that other stuff (v. 5). Some Christians go along like this for years, crowding the Spirit out of their lives, cheating themselves out of spiritual growth.

It's good to take a step back and look at ourselves once in a while, to take stock of where we are and how serious we are about God. You might do this on New Year's or right before Easter or when you have a birthday. James gives several steps to follow: submit to God, resist the Devil, draw near to God, cleanse your hands, purify your heart, get serious, and humble yourself before the Lord (vv. 7–10).

Better yet, don't wait for your birthday. Take time now to talk to God about your spiritual commitment.

Week Twelve: WEDNESDAY

Faith and the Future

Take a Look: James 4:11–17

> *You do not even know what will happen tomorrow.*
> James 4:14

The other day I heard a football player say that his team would be number one for sure next season. Pretty cocky.

It reminded me of San Francisco Giants pitcher Dave Dravecky. Several years ago cancer claimed part of a muscle in his left arm—his throwing arm. Doctors said he'd never pitch a baseball again.

But Dave and his wife believed God could work a miracle. Unbelievably, after a long period of treatment and rehabilitation, Dave came back, pitching some winning games the following season. Then, while pitching against Montreal, Dave's left arm snapped. His miracle was cut short.

What I loved was Dave's attitude. He gave Jesus Christ the credit for healing his arm after the cancer, and after the fracture he told the press, "If God wants me back on the mound, I'll be there." He admitted his total dependence on God.

But the greatest test was yet to come. Doctors detected a return of the cancer, and they had to amputate Dave's arm and shoulder. He went through the usual reactions to a major loss: denial, anger, depression. But with the help of his wife, he finally came to acceptance. He eventually wrote a book, *When You Can't Come Back*, about the whole experience. And he emphasized that his trust in God was stronger than ever.

James tells us, in today's reading, not to be arrogant about the future—we don't know what it will bring (vv. 13–15). He gives the example of the businessman with big plans for the day—and the year—ahead. Sure, it's important to have dreams in life. The people who have accomplished anything significant usually had *big* ones. But we shouldn't get too cocky, as if our success depended on *our* ability and brains alone. Instead, we should be like Dave Dravecky, putting our future in the Lord's hands. After all, God owns it already.

Week Twelve: THURSDAY

Working and Waiting

Take a Look: James 5:1–12

> *See how the farmer waits for the land to yield its valuable crop and how patient he is for the autumn and spring rains.*
>
> *James 5:7*

One semester Miss Summers, my eleventh-grade history teacher, gave us the option of leaving the class for two weeks to work on individual projects in the school library. I decided to write a paper on the stock market crash of 1929. In the library, I quickly found more than enough sources for the paper. But instead of writing, I goofed off—browsing through old *Life* magazines, reading showbiz biographies, and chatting with the librarian. By Thursday of the second week, I hadn't written a word, and Friday was the deadline.

I grabbed all those source books I'd found and spent a frantic Thursday night with a typewriter and a bottle of White-Out. Miss Summers would see that paper exactly as I had composed it at the keyboard.

When I handed it in on Friday, it sure looked like a decent paper. But I knew it was a rush job. I feared the worst when Miss Summers called me to her desk the following week to give me a final grade on my paper. She had her grade book in front of her, and a sinister red pencil in her hand. She was sure to expose me as a fraud.

"Tom, I've reviewed your project," she began. "I've decided to give you a double A, because it was an absolutely superb paper."

I was stunned. Then she continued to praise my paper up and down as I tried not to laugh. When she had finished glowing over my "masterpiece," I returned to my seat.

I was relieved but confused. *A double A?* What had I done to deserve that? My paper wasn't anything special. Miss Summers had simply been fooled by my talent for writing.

It wasn't the first time. Teachers were always giving me extra points on writing assignments, rewarding me for my innate ability to crank stuff out. Only one teacher ever nailed me for faking a paper, and eventually I was able to fool her too. Writing just came easily to me.

The problem was, I thought everything else should come easily. I had very little patience for subjects that didn't: math, science, industrial arts. I didn't know how to really *work* at something. In college I learned, painfully, that my easy skills were only entrance requirements. And my professors weren't easily fooled.

I have friends who were blessed with only average talents but were willing to apply themselves. Today they've achieved more than I; they learned how to work toward goals early on.

In chapter 5, James talks about the farmer, illustrating the importance of *patience*. Like raising crops, getting good at something takes time and effort, and I have to be willing to really work for it over the long haul. I just wish I'd learned it sooner: Mere talent is not enough.

Week Twelve: FRIDAY

Prayer Works

Take a Look: James 5:13–20

> *The prayer of a righteous man is powerful and effective.*
>
> *James 5:16*

Christian author Tony Campolo had just spoken to a large group, when a woman came forward with her son, who was suffering from a crippling leg disorder. She wanted Tony and a pastor who was there to pray for him so he could be healed.

Tony had mixed feelings. Faith healing was really not his thing. But they prayed—hard. And nothing happened. The boy left with braces on his legs. It was a terrible disappointment.

Three years later Campolo met the same woman at a conference. He asked how her son was, expecting the worst.

"He's fine," she said.

"Really? What happened?"

"Well, don't you remember?" she asked, puzzled. "You prayed for him. After that, his legs gradually straightened. Now he's perfectly normal."

Tony kicked himself. It was *her* faith that had allowed the healing, definitely not *his*.

Today's reading reminds us to "pray for each other so that you may be healed." Do you pray only as a last resort? Do you really believe prayer works? James assures us that it does. Maybe the key in praying for healing is to expect a miracle—though not always instantaneously. God can work through the natural processes of the body, over time, and we need to trust him to do that.

Of course, we all know of cases in which prayer seemed to do absolutely nothing. In those cases, God may have a bigger purpose for sickness and suffering. That doesn't mean we should stop praying. At the very least, God's presence will always be there to give courage and comfort to suffering people. And that counts for a whole lot.

Notice that verse 16 says that the prayer of a righteous man can accomplish much. Being righteous means not having a lot of unconfessed sin piling up on your conscience, but it also means making prayer a constant part of your life. Verses 13 and 14 talk about praying when you're cheerful, as well as when you're sick and suffering. The truth is, the more you pray with a clear conscience, the more results you'll see—for yourself and the people you care about. You'll find yourself praying more in line with what God wants for you. And that's when miraculous things can start to happen.

Remember: God wants you to pray so he can act.

Week Twelve: SATURDAY

And I Do Mean Anybody:
Judas Iscariot

Take a Look: John 6:65–71; Matthew 26:1–16

"Have I not chosen you, the Twelve? Yet one of you is a devil!"

John 6:70

OK class, listen up: time for a history lesson.

In 1780, about a year before the end of America's war for independence from Britain, one of George

Washington's generals took command of the fort at West Point, New York.

What was his name?

Anyone?. . .

His name was Benedict Arnold, class.

Arnold was an insecure guy with a thirst for recognition, and a passion for money. He wanted to be *somebody* and live like a king. So he made a deal with the enemy. He would surrender West Point to the British for 20,000 British pounds (a lot of money in those days). When his scheme was exposed, Arnold left West Point and started openly fighting for the British. He was, simply, a *traitor,* hated by everyone loyal to the American cause.

When the war ended, Arnold sailed to Britain. But the rest of his life was a wreck. The British didn't want him any more than the Americans did. He had little money and no respect. But to the very end, he tried to profit from his betrayal.

Judas Iscariot was a traitor, too—one of the big finks of the Bible. You know the story: Judas leads a mob to Jesus at night. Jesus is beaten and dragged before the high priest, the Sanhedrin, and Pontius Pilate and eventually crucified.

And for what? For money—"thirty pieces of silver." As treasurer for Jesus' group, Judas was always thinking about money. In Matthew 26, when a woman anointed Jesus' head with expensive perfume, Judas probably squawked the loudest. "What a waste!" But like the others, he wasn't thinking spiritually. His values were earthbound. Right after the perfume incident, Judas went to the chief priests for his blood money.

Was money Judas' only motive? Hollywood Easter movies, like *The Greatest Story Ever Told,* always look for a way to get Judas off the hook. For instance: *Maybe Judas wanted Jesus hauled in front of the Sanhedrin so he could prove that Jesus was the real Messiah. The plan just went haywire, that's all.*

Sounds reasonable. But we know that it was God's plan all along for his Son to die. And Judas was just the kind of fink needed to get the job done. That's why Jesus chose him.

In his guilt after the Crucifixion, Judas killed himself, and whether he hanged or gored himself to death (Matt. 27:5; Acts 1:16–20), it sure wasn't pretty.

So why include Judas in this book at all? Because there are ways even *Christians* can betray Christ: saying one thing and doing another; saying nothing when you know you should speak up; doing good works for your *own* benefit, instead of Christ's.

Judas Iscariot is proof that God really can use *anybody*—even bad people with selfish motives—to work out his plans. The question is, is that the way *you* want to be used?

WEEK
THIRTEEN

Week Thirteen: SUNDAY

God: No Changes

Take a Look: Psalm 102

> *"You remain the same, and your years will never end."*
> *Psalm 102:27*

Ever notice how some friendships just don't stand the test of time?

I got to know Jill through a Bible study at church. She was sweet and fun; she had lots of energy and liked to laugh. Then she went away to graduate school, and I lost all track of her.

A few years later when Jill was back in town, I ran into her in a little shop downtown. She was . . . different. Still nice, but with a definite *edge*. Her hairstyle was radically different, and she was dressed more grubbily than I had ever seen her. It was good to see her, but I was disappointed. We weren't communicating on the same wavelength anymore. Her graduate school experience had *changed* her.

It was creepy. Here was someone I thought I knew. I thought I had a fix on her personality. I had assumed that she'd always be the same.

How unrealistic can you get? It's perfectly natural for people to change, because we're imperfect. We're influenced by all kinds of things—our friends, our successes, our disappointments. It may make us uncomfortable, but *life changes people*. And as a result, people sometimes drift apart.

That's why it's important to have someone in our lives who *doesn't* change. And God fills the job nicely.

We've looked at a lot of pieces from the puzzle of God's personality over the last twelve weeks—love, grace, holiness, truthfulness, and so forth. Each piece has been absolutely necessary for God to be God. But without this final piece—his changelessness—the others don't mean much.

If God can change, maybe he's been changing ever since the Bible was written. Maybe he really doesn't mean anymore what he said in the Bible. See where this leads us? It leads us to doubt, the opposite of faith.

But God isn't like his creatures. Unlike them, he is perfect—as good as anybody can ever get. So we can depend on him to be himself, forever—in good times and in bad.

That's what the person who wrote Psalm 102 is saying. Even when he was in trouble, even when everything was changing around him, he knew that God would always be the same. God was his rock, his anchor. That gave him hope.

In our last week together, we'll be talking about change, suffering, and the future. It can all be pretty scary. But remember: people and circumstances can change; God never does.

Week Thirteen: MONDAY

Sticking Your Neck Out

Take a Look: Daniel 1

> *But Daniel resolved not to defile himself.*
> *Daniel 1:8*

One day I was sitting around talking with a bunch of non-Christian friends in our high school library. Somebody mentioned a party the previous weekend, where everybody was getting drunk and stoned. I took that opportunity to tell them why, as a Christian, I didn't drink, do drugs, or smoke tobacco. I had learned from experience not to preach too hard on this stuff. I just pointed out that alcohol and drugs were not only bad for your health, they could kill you.

Still, it was really hard. Some of the kids respected me for my convictions, but most of them thought I was just being a weenie. In kind of a mild way, I suppose, I was "suffering for my faith." I was disagreeing with what they were doing, and maybe losing a few friends in the process.

Months later Kathy, one of the girls at the table, told me that because of what I had said that day in the library, she had stopped smoking pot.

"At first I thought you were crazy," she said. "But then I began to wonder, *Why is it that I feel I have to smoke to enjoy myself?* It had become so automatic."

Because I had spoken up, one of my non-Christian friends was thinking about things she hadn't before: about the body God had given her, about her health and her potential. She was seeing that there was another way. That made me feel good. You never can tell what seeds you might be planting in other people's lives.

In today's reading, Daniel and his three friends were part of a special scholarship program. A group of select young men were given the best education and the richest food and wine, to build them up. But Daniel knew that all that rich food and alcohol would hurt more than it would help.

So Daniel got the overseer to agree to a test. And after ten days of eating a healthier diet, Daniel and company not only looked and felt better than the rest, they were a lot sharper mentally too.

This wasn't a happy-ever-after deal for Daniel and his gang, though. They faced real persecution after that—the fiery furnace (Dan. 3) and the lion's den (Dan. 6), among other things. But nobody could argue with their discipline or their willingness to stick their necks out for what they believed. And God took care of them.

Smoking, drinking, drugs, and other unhealthy stuff may be all around you. But good things can come from refusing to go along, and telling people why.

Pray for the courage to stick your neck out for God.

Week Thirteen: TUESDAY

Riding Out the Storm

Take a Look: Romans 8:18–39

> *God works for the good of those who love him.*
> *Romans 8:28*

Two things you can be sure of about suffering. One, it happens to everybody. Two, nobody likes it.

Suffering takes many forms. It can be a single shock, like losing a family member; a daily burden, like a chronic illness or living with someone who is abusive or chemically dependent; or a double whammy—a tragedy hits when we've already got our hands full with everyday problems.

The Bible says a lot about suffering, but sometimes we Christians use the Bible to *explain away* suffering or sweep it under the rug. We offer the Romans 8:28 remedy as a kind of easy spiritual Band-Aid for hurting people.

But to really understand verse 28, you have to read verse 29. The reason bad things "work for good" is because they eventually help to shape us into the likeness of Jesus Christ. This becomes real to you only when you reach the *other side* of suffering, not before. Greater Christlikeness won't come unless you're dealing with your problems here and now, so you can journey on to the other side.

How to do it? Here are some suggestions:

1. Admit that you're suffering and that you don't like it. Obvious? Maybe. But some people are so determined to "keep a stiff upper lip" that they try to ignore the burden they're carrying. That's far more exhausting than facing up to it and getting help.
2. Make God your main resource. When the chips are down, your Bible, prayer time, and ties to church can mean more than ever. God knows

you're hurting and wants to help. Read, pray, think, and be teachable.

3. Easy does it. You may be trying to do too much. If someone you love dies, for example, that's a huge loss. Don't *expect* to be back to your usual routine right away. It's like going back to school too soon when you've had the flu. The extra stress just delays your getting better.

4. Stop destructive behaviors. Ask yourself: "Am I making matters worse?" If possible, stop exposing yourself to sources of pain. If your boyfriend or girlfriend keeps breaking up with you, with more heartache each time, maybe it's time to end your relationship for good. The worst suffering is the kind we inflict on ourselves. Look for ways you're contributing to your own misery, and knock it off.

5. Find someone you can talk to, somebody who's "been there before." An experienced, sympathetic friend can give human eyes, ears, and arms to God's love for you.

6. Be thankful. Even if you're suffering, your life isn't all bad. Thankfulness for the good things puts some perspective on the bad things.

Suffering can lead to a greater resemblance to the Savior. But first things first: Admit the pain. Go to God. Take it easy. Don't make things worse. Talk to someone. Say thanks for the good things.

Week Thirteen: WEDNESDAY

Future Features

Take a Look: 2 Thessalonians 2:1–12

The man of lawlessness is revealed, the man doomed to destruction. He will oppose and will exalt himself

*over everything that is called God or is worshiped, so
that he sets himself up in God's temple, proclaiming
himself to be God.*
                                              2 Thessalonians 2:3–4

Ever wish you could travel through time? Well, you
can't—yet. Movies over this century have supplied us with
a sort of time machine—or more accurately, a crystal ball—
that gives us a sneak preview of coming attractions. But
brace yourself. The picture isn't rosy.

Things to Come

Based on a novel by H. G. Wells, *Things to Come* (1933)
begins in London in 1936. After three decades of war and
pestilence, only gangsters and barbarians survive. A man
named Boss Rudolph intends to lead them in a war against
whatever civilization is left. He is defeated by an elite corps
of airmen called Wings Over the World, which rebuilds London
into a domed Disneyland of high-tech delights.

The Time Machine

Based on the popular novel (H. G. Wells again), this
1960 film has a contraption taking Wells himself (played
by Rod Taylor) eight hundred centuries into the future. He
finds a utopian society populated by healthy, well-fed
young people. The catch? They're only being fattened up
like beef cattle, for the Morlocks, a race of hairy, ill-mannered
cavern dwellers. When a siren sounds, the people walk
trustingly through a door at the base of a huge idol—only
to be shish kebabbed.

Logan's Run

This 1976 movie is about an ingenious "retirement
plan." A society dominated by robots and computers lets
you really live it up until you're thirty—then it's time for
you to pack it in. But you don't get a gold watch; instead,

you're put in a carousel and spun until you break into a billion pieces. No wonder Logan was running.

Notice the theme that keeps cropping up in these films? A force beyond ourselves threatens to dominate and destroy us. The moviemakers may have been smarter than they knew; even the Bible predicts this will happen.

In 2 Thessalonians 2, Paul says that in the last days, one man (the *Antichrist*) will rule the world and try to become God (vv. 3–4). On earth will be a time of *tribulation*—turmoil, death, and suffering. Not to worry, though. Jesus Christ will come back and end this world ruler's reign (v. 8).

Remember: There really is a spiritual battle going on, and it will eventually heat up big time. But people who trust Christ as their Savior are on the winning side, with guaranteed reservations for a trip beyond time and trouble, into eternity.

Week Thirteen: THURSDAY

Gimme Heaven

Take a Look: Revelation 21:9–22:5

> *And he . . . showed me the Holy City, Jerusalem, coming down out of heaven from God. It shone with the glory of God.*
>
> *Revelation 21:10–11*

"Heaven is a wonderful place." That's the first line of a chorus I used to sing with my youth group. As Christians, we were confident that our afterlife would be wonderful, even though we knew very little about it.

A recent survey revealed that *most* Americans believe in heaven and in hell too, for that matter—78 percent for heaven, 60 percent for hell. But *what* do they believe? There are a lot of popular myths about heaven out there.

For instance, some people believe that life in heaven will be *dull*. They reason that when we die and go to heaven, "the game is over." We spend our lives on earth working, learning, growing, and facing challenges. But in heaven everything will be perfect, effortless. There will be no meaning to a life with no obstacles to overcome or goals to achieve and no sin to spice things up. We'll have the world on a golden platter. Then what?

This just shows our puny thinking. Ask yourself: Why would God create the world and give human beings free will, only to see them disobey him and have to start over after the Flood? Why would he make Israel his chosen people and give them the Ten Commandments, only to see them broken? Why would he give them a Messiah, only to see him crucified? Send apostles to evangelize the world, only to see them killed for the sake of the gospel? Send the Spirit to create the church, only to see the church stray from him? Reform the church, only to see it persecuted by an unbelieving world in the end times? Why? Why would he go to all that trouble and pain? So that folks can go to heaven and sit around on a cloud, doing nothing?

Of course not. God has been up to something much more important, all along—*setting up his kingdom.* He has been patiently working through human history to allow his creatures to participate in that kingdom—a place where the chief activity will be knowing and worshiping him.

Faith in Jesus Christ makes us citizens in this great kingdom, and it will be anything but dull. Today's Scripture reading describes a real place—large, bright, and colorful. A place of wonder, peace, and plenty. In eternity, with no sense of time, we'll have plenty of room for creative activities. We won't be weighed down by physical imperfections. We'll have unlimited potential to build on the foundation of our earthly lives. We won't just *be* with God;

we'll *reign* with him. Our faithfulness to Christ in this life will determine our reward in heaven. But none of us will be sorry we came.

Heaven *is* a wonderful place, where we'll have the chance to know God fully and finally become who he meant us to be all along. Hope to see you there!

Week Thirteen: FRIDAY

The Other Place

Take a Look: 2 Thessalonians 1:3–12; Revelation 20:11–15

> *They will be punished with everlasting destruction and shut out from the presence of the Lord and from the majesty of his power.*
>
> *2 Thessalonians 1:9*

Now for the bad news. While the Bible speaks of heaven, a place of eternal bliss, it also speaks of hell—a place of eternal punishment, torment, and general unpleasantness. This is also a real place, where real things happen to real persons. It is a place reserved for people who have rejected Christ and defiantly decided to live only for themselves. These people will be identified and judged before God's "great white throne" at the end of time.

One of the best-known descriptions of hell comes not from the Bible but from classical literature. Dante's *Inferno* goes into imaginative detail about a multilevel place of destruction that spirals down, down, down, with all kinds of creative punishments along the way. One particular evil-doer was locked in a metal cage suspended over fire, while flames intermittently shot through him, and the cage prevented his escape. That was to be his fate for all eternity.

Creative? Yes. Grim? To be sure. But a little too color-ful, even for the Bible. Because the Word of God doesn't get overly specific about what hell is like or what punishments are in store.

We do know, from the Bible, that hell is described as a fiery place of judgment. "If anyone's name was not found written in the book of life, he was thrown into the lake of fire" (Rev. 20:15). But Jesus also called it a place of separa-tion, when he said that unbelievers would be cast "outside, into the darkness, where there will be weeping and gnash-ing of teeth" (Matt. 8:12). In 2 Thessalonians Paul said that people who disobeyed the gospel would be "punished with everlasting destruction and shut out from the presence of the Lord and from the majesty of his power" (1:9).

Fire? Darkness? Destruction? It all points to a place where you'd rather not end up. The cost of unbelief means eternal separation from the loving presence of God. To be left alone with one's guilty conscience for eternity would be "fire" enough.

The good news is, you have to *choose* to go to hell—by rejecting God's love for you. But you can also *choose* to trust Christ and live with him forever. When you think about it, that's really no choice at all.

Week Thirteen: SATURDAY

God Can Use Anybody, Final Chapter: Paul

Take a Look: Acts 9:1–22; 1 Corinthians 15:9–11

By the grace of God I am what I am.
1 Corinthians 15:10

The U.S. Supreme Court banned involuntary prayer and Bible reading in public schools in 1963. It was the result of a successful lawsuit brought by Madalyn Murray O'Hair, the famous atheist, and her son, Bill Murray, a high school student.

Bill was raised to believe that God didn't exist and to hate anything religious. In his twenties, he worked with his mother on a bunch of new lawsuits—against tax-exempt status for churches; against the phrase *In God We Trust,* embossed on our coins; and against the words *under God,* used in the pledge of allegiance.

But Bill started having serious doubts about atheism. In his mother he saw a bitter, negative, and destructive woman who had controlled and abused him. He was depressed and eventually became an alcoholic. In a treatment program, he met people whose lives had been transformed by faith. He started opening up to God and finally made a commitment to Christ. Today he's an evangelist! Bill had fought God every step of the way. But he couldn't resist him forever.

That's Paul's story in a nutshell. He started out as Saul, a rising young star among the Pharisees, making brownie points by having followers of Jesus rounded up, put in prison, and even killed. In Acts 9 he was on his way to Damascus to hammer some believers there. He was determined to squash Christianity.

So when Saul had a life-changing close encounter with Christ, he was as surprised as anybody. But out of his dramatic conversion, Saul became Paul and traveled his world, preaching the gospel.

He couldn't have known, at first, what he was getting into. In his travels he was whipped, beaten, and stoned for his faith. He was shipwrecked three times and was robbed. He was sleepless, cold, and hungry in countless places. But of all the apostles, Paul probably worked the hardest and accomplished the most. And he gave God all the credit for what he was able to do: "By the grace of God I am what I am" (1 Cor. 15:10). He had weaknesses and limitations, but he was one of the greatest Christians of all time.

Bill Murray and Paul the apostle are maybe the best proof of what I've been saying for the last thirteen Saturdays: No matter who you are, no matter what you've done or how you've failed, God wants you. He wants you to come to him, to know him, to love him, to live for him. Don't resist—it's your greatest chance in life to do something big. When you look at the sorry bunch Jesus started with, you should be encouraged.

God can use anybody. Let him use you.

We want to hear from you. Please send your comments about this
book to us in care of the address below. Thank you.

ZondervanPublishingHouse
Grand Rapids, Michigan 49530
http://www.zondervan.com